Already Pretty

Learning to Love Your Body by Learning to Dress It Well

By Sally McGraw

D1275359

ISBN-13: 978-1475148275
ISBN-10: 1475148275
Library of Congress Catalog Card Number: 2012906251

Visit **www.alreadypretty.com** for more information about the author, to participate in online
forums related to this book, and to purchase a companion PDF.

This book is dedicated to Ellen Esrick
who believed in me as a writer
when I was only eight years old.

Huge thanks to my husband, Mike McGraw,
who contributes daily from behind the scenes.
To my parents, Dan and Stephanie Weinbach,
whose support and encouragement have been steadfast.
To Barbara Moore, Jen Larson, and Annie Wilder,
my amazing mentors, without whom this book
would have remained unwritten.
To Christina Holm-Sandok for allowing me to
photograph her gorgeous closet and wardrobe.
To Deanna Raybourn, Elissa Stern, and Brenda Ulrich
for their invaluable advice and guidance.
To the marvelous group of bloggers
whose photos are featured in this book.

And to my amazing blog readers, whose kindness and
generosity overwhelms me on a daily basis.

Table of Contents

Introduction

I used to spend so much energy hating my body that I exhausted myself into depression. For years I employed fad diets and constant exercise to fight my physical form, convinced that my body's shape and size were the root of my misery. And although my weight would fluctuate when I made these drastic changes, I maintained the same basic figure, which I continued to hate.

It wasn't until I began exploring personal style—dressing in fun, flattering, form-fitting clothes—that an unexplored universe slowly revealed itself. As I started buying clothing and accessories that drew the eye to my tiny waist, my shapely shoulders, and my delicate ankles, I could feel my lifelong hatred beginning to ebb. I realized that clothes were tools and that putting those tools to good use made me feel marvelous. And for the first time, I respected my body. I realized there was nothing *wrong* with my body. I accepted my body as integral to my identity. Suddenly I wanted to show it off, decorate it joyously, and hone my personal style so that I could understand it on new levels. When I started to dress in a way that made me look and feel amazing, I finally stopped actively, continually, exhaustingly hating my body. And I immediately wanted to show other women how to make that same connection, so they could stop hating theirs.

With that goal in mind, I started writing about the intersection of style and body image on my blog, Already Pretty, and have done so every day for nearly five years. I've taught countless women to dress to their strengths, embrace their natural figures, and express themselves through personal style. And in turn, they've taught me that the vast majority of style resources available to creative, curious women are inadequate and badly broken. These books, magazines, and TV programs push women to create tall, thin, balanced figures, but never offer any alternatives. They convince women that style is hard and that they're doing it wrong. They indicate that any fashion problem can be fixed if enough money is thrown at it, and they seldom recommend utilizing the external and internal resources that a woman has at hand.

Many style guides shame women about their bodies, cow them into believing they must disguise their natural forms, and attempt to force them into a single, rigid stylistic mold. But it doesn't have to be that way. Stylish dressing can be highly individual, friendly to all figures, and deliciously creative. When women are taught to dress expressively and personally, they link looking good in their clothing to feeling good about their bodies. I believe the time has come for a style guide that focuses on the personal instead of the general. I believe the time has come for a style guide that embraces physical *and* sartorial diversity. And I believe the time has come for a style guide that will trust women, empower them, and transform them.

So I wrote one.

Style should be personal. It should be an expression of your inner self projected outward to the observing world. Style should suit your body. It should highlight the aspects of your physical form that make you swell with pride. Style should be accessible to all women, not just those already inclined to be fashion-forward, trend-savvy, well-groomed creatures. And perhaps most importantly, style should empower all women, not just those who fit the current tall, thin, balanced beauty-body paradigm.

And it absolutely can! Clothes may have been invented to keep you warm and hide your private bits from prying eyes, but the reason they exist in such variety is to help you look amazing. And you can look amazing, no matter how you're built.

You don't need to fear style. Clothes are vehicles for self-expression, and there is no wrong way to express yourself. You don't need a whole new wardrobe to be stylish. Working with what you've already got will help you craft a personal style that suits your unique tastes. You don't need to look a certain way to be gorgeous and chic and fashion-forward. It's a diverse world, and there's room in it for your unique brand of personal style.

In this book, I'm going to explain why cultivating personal style is important work, integral to loving and accepting yourself completely. Then I'll walk you through defining the style you're sporting right now, identifying key wardrobe staples from your very own closet. I'll help you pinpoint figure-flattery priorities based on your own preferences and help you discard any antiquated ones fueled by unattainable cultural ideals. I'll encourage you to mull over your ideal style and show you how to merge it with your current style. I'll lead, but you'll do the brunt of the work. Using steps I've devised, tested, and outlined, you'll transform your personal style and work toward using that style to celebrate your beauty.

And if you take all of my ideas to heart, you'll learn to dress for the woman you are right now, today, in this shape, size, and configuration. You'll learn to shake off your sartorial fears and craft a style that is truly your own. You'll learn to accept clothes as tools, and you'll be able to reach into that toolbox, rummage around a little, and extract something flattering, renewing, and empowering.

And once you've done that, you'll see you don't need a different body to be beautiful. Because you're already pretty.

LuAnne, Weesha's World
weeshasworld.com

Chapter 1: Why Style?

Fashion can be scary. It often involves impossibly high heels, impossibly expensive handbags, and impossibly odd garments. Fashion can be exclusionary. Most high-end designers don't manufacture garments above a US size 10 or 12, and most of those garments won't work on anything other than the curve-free body of a runway model. Fashion can be judgmental and unyielding, harsh and intimidating, overwhelming and limiting.

Luckily, this is not a fashion book.

This book will not badger you into wearing the season's trendiest items. This book will not make you into a carbon copy of some generic fashionable femme. This book will not force you to abandon your ballet flats in favor of sky-scraping Louboutins. (Although it will help you find the courage to do so, if that's what you want to do.)

And, above all, this book will not force fashion down your throat because fashion is far too impersonal. Fashion focuses on the clothes while ignoring the wearer. But style? Style is personal, emotional, unique. Style is created by an individual with tastes, needs, and a specific set of curves and angles. Style is an aesthetic evolution, an engaging, ongoing process of exploration and discovery. And style can be a remarkably effective tool for cultivating a healthy, positive body image. Truly, it can.

Now, there are a million different paths to self-love, and no one is quicker, better, or more effective than the others. There are a million different ways to bolster your body image, and all of them are worth exploring. So why am I encouraging you to consider personal style as a means to transform your self-image? Why do I see clothing as a valuable tool for cultivating positive body image? Why is style important?

MERE TRAPPINGS

Most women have complex relationships with their bodies. These relationships can be difficult to change and often center on socially reinforced ideas of beauty, weight, fitness,sexuality, and attractiveness that drain natural stores of confidence. Many women who realize they are struggling with poor body image opt to work on these issues by eradicating or rerouting unhealthy thought patterns. But others may prefer to take more concrete action.

Concrete action often means changing diet and exercise habits, considering plastic or gastrointestinal surgery, or other choices that may lead to changes to the body itself. Women are taught to feel dissatisfied with their natural forms and trained to believe that *changing* those forms will lead to happiness and self-acceptance. But the belief that our bodies are "wrong" and need correcting is a form of self-loathing in and of itself. And, perhaps more importantly, there are other ways to improve body image that don't involve altering your body's size or shape.

Making changes to your wardrobe and style can affect how you view your body, even if your body itself hasn't changed. Throwing on a skirt that works with your curves instead of against them allows you to embrace those curves. Slipping on a fantastic pair of boots can illustrate that those legs are damned fine just as they are. Finding styles, colors, and textures that enhance your natural assets can help you see how gorgeous you are right now and have been all along. Just by changing the clothing, shoes, and accessories that adorn your body, you can change your relationship with that body for the better. Minus the oppressive workout plan, restrictive diet, and nip/tuck.

INSIDE OUT

Many children are gripped by an irrepressible desire to broadcast their personal passions. They wear character- and slogan-emblazoned tee shirts, paper their bedroom walls and locker doors with photos and drawings, and covet merchandise associated with their favorite stories, sports teams, products, and ideas. They want *everyone* to understand their loves and obsessions. Everyone. And although their actions are often related to peer acceptance, group identification, and social norms, those actions also represent the beginnings of self-expression and definition.

As kids become adults, the constant desire to display personal passions fades away. But many grown-ups still yearn to communicate select information about their personalities, and style can be a fantastic outlet for expressing the inner self to the outer world. Wearing maxi skirts, bangles, and crochet accents can hint at Bohemian roots. Choosing an all black palette broken up by buckles, sequins, and studs creates an alluring toughness. Relying on ruffled blouses and antique jewelry as style staples expresses an inner romanticism. Even fabric, color, and texture choices are likely to give astute observers a bit of information about the wearer's tastes and preferences.

Audi, Fashion for Nerds
geekthreads.blogspot.com

You dress and groom your body, so you alone are in charge of how you appear to observers. You get to choose what to express and what to hide, what to display and what to mask. It's a lot of power, don't you think? Since you've got to get dressed anyway, why not take the opportunity to broadcast a few key pieces of information about yourself to the observing world? Doing so can build pride and confidence, establish your uniqueness, and help you decide which aspects of your inner life you'd like to highlight and share.

Gracey, Fashion for Giants
fashionforgiants.blogspot.com

CYCLES OF RESPECT

If you wish to earn the respect of others, your best bet is to broadcast respect for yourself. After all, you can hardly expect people to admire, trust, and esteem you if you don't feel confident in your abilities, proud of your accomplishments, and capable of handling life's surprises. Since feeling respected by others builds self-confidence, and appearing confident garners respect, all you've got to do is kick-start the process, which will perpetuate itself.

One of the easiest ways to broadcast respect for yourself is to dress with care. Comportment, demeanor, dress, grooming, and overall appearance constitute the first levels of information about ourselves that we offer to the observing world. They may not be the most important, but they are the first, which makes them worthy of effort and attention. You cannot control eye color or proportions or height, but you can control behavior, cleanliness, and personal style. And while we've already proven those to be channels for self-expression, they can also become channels for broadcasting self-respect.

Dressing with care does not mean suits or heels or flat-ironed hair. Not to everyone. Dressing with care does not mean skirts instead of jeans, slicked-back hair instead of loose waves, or designer clothes instead of thrift finds. Not to everyone. Dressing with care means finding clothing that fits and suits your unique figure, giving thought to the day's activities and participants before choosing your ensemble, and selecting garments that make you feel comfortable, powerful, proud, and truly yourself. Dressing with care will look different on every single one of us, and that is a marvelous good thing. But dressing with care also means the same thing to us all: making sartorial choices that showcase our best selves.

When we dress to show respect for ourselves, people around us cannot help but sense our confidence. If you want others to respect you, you must respect yourself first. And show it.

THE LOOK GOOD-FEEL GOOD CONNECTION

When you're feeling kinda wretched about the current state of your body, you tend to lose interest in shopping. And eventually, shopping apathy can morph into diminished interest in clothes. And sometimes *that* indifference becomes an inability to engage in basic grooming.

It's a fun little cycle, and oftentimes you've gotta hit bottom to shake loose severe body blues. A candid party photo of your unkempt self that gives you the shivers, a cutting comment from a coworker, or something equally traumatic can throw your long-rusted self-care gears in the opposite direction.

Now consider this: what if you forced it? What if—on those days when you looked in the mirror and saw Grendel—you made yourself don a flirty frock, curl your hair, and slip on a sassy set of heels? Would it help or hurt how you felt about your body and face and overall self?

We've already established that the cycle of self-loathing is inextricably linked to the cycle of self-neglect: feel bad, look bad, feel worse, look worse, and on and on. But I maintain that a cycle of self-love can be perpetuated by a cycle of self-care. If you feel awful about how you look and allow yourself to look as awful as you feel, you spiral down. But if you feel awful about how you look and work against that negativity—beautifying yourself with the tools you have at hand—you can spiral up.*

When you put effort into your appearance, you are less likely to hide from mirrors, eat nothing but crap, and withdraw from social situations. When you put effort into your appearance, you are more likely to receive compliments—important sources of external

*While I certainly believe in style as an instrument of self-care, I also know that some blues are more than just blues. No flirty dress or pair of heels will cure clinical depression. Don't be afraid to ask for help when you need it.

feedback that encourage you to *continue* putting effort into your appearance. When you put effort into your appearance, you don't wallow, you move.

Caring about how you present your physical self to the world makes you more present in your body. Presence in your body feeds itself, creating more care. The cycle of self-care feeding self-love creating more self-care allows you to broadcast a profile of self-respect and power. It reminds you that you can control how you feel about yourself. And that's powerful good stuff.

You can use personal style as a tool to cultivate self-care and reflect self-respect. No matter how tall you are or where you carry the most jiggle, you can learn to flatter your figure. You can utilize your natural, perfect beauty to reflect your undeniably amazing self outward to the observing world. And when you do, you kick-start the machinery of self-love.

Keri, Headlines & Hemlines
headlinesandhemlines.com

Bottom line: making changes to or refining your personal style is an accessible, concrete, relatively speedy way to begin changing how you view your body without changing the body itself. Your style can help you express your tastes, build self-respect, gain the respect of others, and cultivate positive feelings about your overall appearance.

Again, style is not the only or best way to transform self-image. But it's a good one. So if you feel that revising your personal style could help you learn to accept and love your beautiful body just as it is, let's do this thing.

The remainder of this book will walk you through a process of examination, evaluation, and refinement. Since I can't crawl through the pages to guide you through the process personally, I'm giving you the tools and showing you the steps so you can, essentially, make *yourself* over. There are lots of tasks and exercises. You'll create your very own, customized personal style guidebook. You'll mull and write and revisit. You will make lists, take photos, and donate ill-fitting clothes to your favorite charities.

As you move through these steps, you'll begin to understand your current style and decide which aspects of it will remain constant while you tweak and change others. You'll examine the importance of figure flattery and learn what makes certain garments more flattering than others. You'll identify your own figure-flattery priorities and decide how to fit them into your personal style. You'll identify and refine your ideal style, evaluating your current wardrobe pieces and choosing potential new style staples. Then you'll work to merge your current style with your ideal, creating a blend that allows you to maintain select aspects of your established sartorial identity while simultaneously introducing new or refined ones. It's a ton of work, no two ways about it. But if you commit to it, are honest throughout, and tackle the process one chunk at a time, you'll be absolutely amazed by what you'll learn. And by how chic, aware, and empowered you feel when it's all done.

First off: we're gonna take a stab at defining your current style.

TOOLS AND SUPPORT

The work you undertake as you move through this book will be fascinating, engaging, and important. It might also feel a bit overwhelming at times. If you have questions as you go through the process, hit a wall, need support, or just want to talk to others who are doing the same work, visit **alreadypretty.com** and click on "forums." You'll find a thread dedicated to each chapter in this book, so you can compare notes with other readers.

Patty, The Snug Bug
pattythesnugbug.com

18

Chapter 2: Defining Your Current Style

TOOLS YOU'LL NEED:
Three folders
Computer with Internet access
Computer printer
Blank journal or notebook
Poster board and glue (optional)
Camera (optional)

Now that you've committed to revamping your personal style, it's tempting to dive right into purging your closet and buying armloads of new duds, isn't it? RESIST THE URGE, my friend. Before you can choose a new sartorial destiny, you need to assess your current style. And that will take something that's rarely allotted to personal style: time.

Think about it: most people spend ten minutes per day thinking about style, clothing, and outfit assembly. Those ten minutes are typically spent staring, panic-stricken, at the contents of a messy closet, wondering if nudity is a viable option for the day's tasks. Dedicating some time and energy to defining and understanding your current dressing preferences is an important step in your personal style journey. If you don't learn your stylistic history, you'll be doomed to repeat it.

So, how do you go about defining your current style?

RESEARCH

Very few women can describe their personal dressing styles in short, descriptive phrases. The ones who can either spent some serious time and energy considering the question, or they are fancy celebrities who've been interviewed by multiple fashion magazines. Formulating a catchy phrase that encapsulates your style isn't strictly necessary, but *understanding* your current style is absolutely required. And to do that, you're gonna need some folders.

Start with the visuals: collect any current photographs of yourself that showcase typical outfits or outfit elements. Harvest them from scrapbooks, smartphone cameras, Facebook, anywhere at all. If you don't have any photos that reflect your current style, consider taking a few self-portraits in the mirror. Print everything out and stick it all in a folder.

Then spend some time studying other women's styles to identify a few who dress similarly to you. Explore group-driven photo collectives like Chictopia (chictopia.com), Pinterest (pinterest.com), and the Wardrobe Remix group on Flickr (flickr.com/groups/wardrobe_remix/). Investigate a few personal style blogs to see if any bloggers are sporting styles similar to yours.* Try not to focus on physical attributes but instead on sartorial similarities. Find women who wear your colors, your dress styles, your shoe types, your accessories. Also try to remember that you're seeking women who dress as you do, right now, today. You'll gravitate toward gals whose style you admire and want to emulate, but do your best to push that instinct aside. Concentrate on the now. Once you've found some images of women whose styles resemble your own current style, print 'em out and stick 'em in another folder.

* If you aren't a blog reader, start at Wardrobe Remix and Chictopia since many of the community members are also bloggers. Click through to any member blogs that seem interesting and explore those bloggers' blogrolls for other relevant blogs. Then say aloud all variations of the word "blog" until your lips go numb.

Finally, identify a style icon—someone whose style has inspired you in the past or whose style has some overlap with your own. Celebrities are the most common choices, but feel free to pick a friend, relative, or coworker instead. Again, do your best to select someone who is influencing you now as opposed to someone who dresses how you wish you could dress. If possible, collect a few photos. You guessed it—folder them.

Ideally, you should take all of these images, cut them out, and paste them on a giant piece of poster board. Make a collage that illustrates your present-day style. Seeing a large group of photos that represent various elements of your own style, laid out together, will help you distill your thoughts and ideas about that style. But if the thought of undertaking such an art project makes you cringe, just keep your folders handy. You'll need them for your next task.

WRITE

Writing helps us crystallize our ideas. When we write, we are forced to articulate nebulous thoughts, define the parameters of our beliefs, assign details, and refine meanings. If writing isn't easy for you, fear not. The writing you'll do as you explore your personal style can remain private forever. But forcing yourself to do it will help you process and refine, distill and explore your thoughts about style, body, and self.

Invest a few bucks in a blank journal, notebook, or small scrapbook. If you're a tech whiz, you could create an electronic document in the word processing program of your choice. This will become your Style Journal, the repository of your dressing-related ideas.

Start this new journal with a list of adjectives that describe your current style. Generate as many as you can, but aim for at least ten. Are you trendy, classic, arty, romantic, eclectic, or punk? Do you feel bold, soft, edgy, or funky? Are your clothes colorful, boxy, diaphanous, fitted, or retro? Try to be as specific as possible, and do your best to create balance in your list. If you believe that your current style is frumpy, outdated, or uncool, include those words but note some of the positives alongside the negatives.

Next, jot down and answer these style-centric questions in your journal, referring to your photo collage as needed:

1. What clothing brands do you love to wear? Why?
2. What clothing brands do you hate? Why?
3. What's your go-to outfit? (A tee shirt and jeans? A dress and heels? A sweater and slacks?)
4. What styles do you love to wear? (Think in terms of garments: styles of blouse, sweater, skirt, dress, pant, shoe, etc.)
5. What styles do you wish you could wear?
6. What styles do you think look horrendous on you? In what ways do they fight your figure?
7. What are your favorite colors?
8. What are your favorite patterns? (If any.)
9. What are your favorite fabrics?
10. Are you a skirt girl, pants girl, or both?
11. Do you wear dresses? If so, what style?
12. What styles of shoes you like? Do you own shoes in those styles?
13. Can you wear heels? Do you enjoy wearing heels?
14. What accessories do you wear most often? (Scarves, belts, watches, hosiery, etc.)
15. Which pieces of jewelry do you wear most often? (Earrings, necklaces, bracelets, brooches, etc.)
16. What motivates you to shop? Do you enjoy shopping?
17. Is there an era of fashion that you absolutely adore?

Write as much or as little as you'd like for each answer, but take a stab at every single one of these questions. They'll help you sketch out the underlying structure of your personal style.

Compose a list of your most-worn items. Grab your Style Journal, head over to your closet, and peek inside. Which garments, accessories, and shoes are in constant rotation? Note each one and jot down some reasons why these favorites get so much use. Are they comfortable? Flattering? Versatile? Durable? Washable? What traits make these items your personal wardrobe staples?

Finally, assess constants and changes. What aspects of your current style do you hope to maintain? Have you refined your color palette? Do you know how to rock colorful tights? Are you happy with your overall preppy/minimalist/trendy vibe and hope to stick to it? It's unlikely that you'll want to overhaul everything, so take a moment to identify a few constants. Then consider which aspects of your current style you hope to change. Would you rather focus on skirts and dresses, less on jeans and pants? Do you need to expand your shoe wardrobe? Are you looking to dress more playfully?

Once you've tackled these four brain-benders, step away. Close your Style Journal and don't think about it for a week or two. This kind of self-analysis should happen as organically as possible and rushing the process will cause you to burn out and give up.

STYLE JOURNAL SIDE NOTE: PERSONALIZATION

As you work your way through this book, you'll see that the Style Journal gets a lot of airtime. Although it may sound like a major hassle to create a style-focused journal with gobs of handwritten information about your preferences and insights, you'll discover that the time and effort you invest in this tool will pay off. And then some.

Some things to consider as you dive into personalizing your Style Journal:

- If you worry about introducing errors and having to scribble them out, consider an inexpensive spiral-bound notebook. That way, if a page becomes riddled with errors, you can easily rip it out and start fresh.

- If you're a visual thinker, consider a journal with blank pages so you can sketch ideas or paste photographs into relevant sections. But try not to fall in love with an oversized model; eventually, you'll want to tote this journal with you as you shop, so it should fit inside your preferred day bag.

- Although I highly recommend longhand, you can certainly create an electronic Style Journal. A document on a laptop or tablet can serve just as well as a paper journal, and it allows for easy editing and access. Do try to keep your journal in a portable device, though, as it helps to bring it into your actual closet for certain tasks and along for future shopping trips.

Many exercises and tasks from this book will go inside your Style Journal, but feel free to add any additional customizations or insights that feel appropriate. This is your tool. It should feel right to you and only you.

If you find that the prospect of undertaking a longhand or electronic journal is just too much, I've created a printable PDF workbook that will walk you through the basics. Visit **alreadypretty.com** to purchase and download the PDF.

Then, when you feel ready, crack open that sucker and read over what you wrote. Does it ring true? Anything need tweaking? If you feel like you've painted a fairly accurate picture of your current style, attempt to boil it down.

Describe your current style in a single phrase. After much rumination, I've come to describe my own style as "arty eclectic with a broad streak of retro influence." My friend Sarah's style is "fancy weirdo." (Check her out at yesandyes.org.) I'd describe Katie Holmes's style as "equal parts elegant classics and edgy trends." Consider everything you've learned about your style so far and try to encapsulate it in a single concise, descriptive phrase. Write it down in your Style Journal.

OR

Fill in these blanks: My style is currently _____, _____, and _____. I wish it were more

_____ and less _____. Most days I wear _____. I look my best in _____.

Feels pretty good, am I right? One of the most important steps in honing your personal style is to understand its roots and quirks and boundaries. You're well on your way now, lady.

PLAY

So, you've done some important preliminary thinking and writing, taken a little break to let your brain breathe, and come back to home in on the core of your personal style. Now let's move away from all that introspective stuff and dig into some outfit assembly, shall we? Since we're still focused on your current style, we're going to work with what you've already got on hand. Grab your Style Journal and head over to the closet.

Pull out your top five most-worn items and spread them on your bed. Don't limit yourself to clothing! If you've got a pair of shoes that work their way into three outfits per week, plunk those down, too. Now challenge yourself to assemble an outfit around each of these faves. No need to focus on crafting unusual ensembles or bringing underutilized items into the mix. Just whip up five outfits based on your top five wardrobe workhorses – right down to the jewelry and accessories – and try them on. When you're done, jot down the outfit elements in your Style Journal. Or, if you're feeling enterprising, snap a photo of the outfit to print out and add to your journal. Once you're done documenting, put everything back into the closet.

Pull out your top five least-worn items and spread them on your bed. Ahhh, now things are getting interesting. To be clear: I want you to pull items that you don't wear but still fit,

suit, and please you. The threadbare concert tee that's stuck around for sentimental reasons doesn't qualify. Choose pieces you don't but *could* wear often, closet orphans just waiting for their moment to shine. Now challenge yourself to assemble an outfit around each of these items and try on the assembled outfits to make sure they really work. More often than not, pieces fall into neglect when they don't fit naturally into our usual outfit styles and formulas. Simply dragging them out and using them as starting points can clarify their place in the larger wardrobe. Once you've crafted your five outfits, note the pieces in your Style Journal or snap some quick photos. Put everything away.

Workshop ten additional outfits, utilizing items from your closet. That may sound daunting, but it's a lot more manageable than you might think. Include your absolute favorite outfit as well as a few others down the gradient: an outfit you like but aren't sure flatters you, an outfit you wear all of the time but that isn't really "you," an outfit that you like but aren't totally comfortable wearing. When you run out of standby outfits, try the same technique you used in the previous two tasks: start with a single item and build around it. The purpose of this exercise is to get you to think about which items are useful, which ones make you feel comfortable or beautiful or strong, and which ones really belong in your closet. Try these outfits on, so they move beyond theory and into practice. Jot down the details in your Style Journal, or take photos. Put everything away.

You can revisit these three exercises any time you're suffering from wardrobe malaise. If your closet looks like a blur of boring and you cannot seem to coax forth a single inspired outfit, take some time to walk through these steps on a weekend afternoon and see if it helps. Again, most people spend ten panic-stricken minutes per day considering outfit assembly. Carving out time for a more considered review of your wardrobe will reveal many promising ensembles. It will! And now: The purge. (Dun dun duuuunnnnnnnn…)

EVALUATE

Even people who love purging their closets also hate purging their closets. Clothing is imbued with emotion, steeped in memory, and parting with it can be downright painful. As

rewarding as it feels to jettison long-languishing items, it can be stressful to part with pants that will never fit again, gifts from long-lost loves, expensive duds you never wore.

I'm not gonna tell you to invite your girlfriends over, open a bottle of wine, and make a party of it. You certainly can, but for many women, closet purges are extremely personal and most effective when undertaken alone. Regardless of whether you tackle the task on your own or with help, promise me you'll make time for it. Real time. Do not purge your closet in between other tasks over the course of a month. Set aside a full weekend day, hire a sitter, banish everyone. It sounds like overkill, but you will not regret carving out the space and time for this task. Promise.

Start with your neglected, underutilized, and languishing items. Try them on. Yes, all of them. Including shoes and accessories. Yes, I know it's going to take ages. Remember, you've got all day. Try them on in a well-lit room in front of a full-length mirror.

1. **If an item never fit in the first place, donate it.** You should begin dressing for your today body as soon as possible. Clothing that never worked with your figure damages your body image. Donate it to a worthy cause.

2. **If an item shames you for your body shape or shopping habits, sell it.** If an item has negative associations, recouping your losses can soften the parting blow. Consign, sell oneBay, or find some other way to make a few of your bucks back.

3. **If an item's value is emotional, store it or document it.** You can keep the shredded jeans from your carefree days in high school, but you don't need to store them in your active closet. If you can't bear to part with them, find an obliging corner of your basement. If you don't have much storage space, photograph or journal about the item before you send it along to a new home.

4. **If it is damaged, repair it.** Some items are neglected because they're broken. Replace buttons, have shoes resoled, take ill-fitting items to the tailor.

5. **If you love it but don't know how to wear it, display it prominently.** Many items remain neglected simply because they're hidden from view. Move challenging items to the front of the closet so you can see them.

Don't feel obliged to jettison everything that is currently too big or small for you. Bodies fluctuate. Many women's bodies fluctuate on a monthly basis and having some size options on hand can be incredibly helpful. But consider these two important things before deciding to hang on to any article of clothing that doesn't fit your today body:

• **Are you being honest?** It makes sense to hang on to jeans a size or two away from your current size in case of weight changes. But beyond that may be pushing reason. While you may return to a previous size someday, remember that you can replace virtually all clothing. You should donate items that are far smaller or larger than you are now. Letting them go can help you accept your body and move toward loving it.

• **Are you hurt by their presence?** Memories of other body shapes and sizes can be painful for a multitude of reasons. Any items of clothing that prompt feelings of disappointment, shame, or self-loathing don't belong in your closet, or in your house. Find them new homes for those pieces and focus on the clothing that inspires, beautifies, and energizes you.

Now that you've sussed out your least-worn items, let's move on to your most-worn pieces. Try them on. Yes, all of them. Now ask yourself:

1. **What is their relationship to your current style?** Some frequently worn items may fit into your current style but feel stale or tired. Consider jettisoning those or placing them into storage until you've made more decisions about where your style is headed. Keep anything that feels classic or quintessentially "you."

2. **Do they make you look good *and* feel good?** Ideal garments will work with your body. That means they'll highlight your favorite attributes without causing you acute discomfort. Items that feel great but look awful should be reserved for sick days. Items that look great but feel awful should be ejected from your closet. Some garments will fall more on the "look good" or "feel good" side of the fence, of course, and that's fine. But always consider your compromises. Carefully.

3. **If they're keepers, do they need repair or replacement?** Wardrobe staples are among the items most likely to show wear and tear. How are yours holding up? If they are items that you know will endure beyond any style revisions, make sure they're in good shape.

That probably took a while. If you were as thorough as you should've been, you've just tried on and evaluated everything in your closet.

If you're on the brink of exhaustion, call it a day. If you've got any energy left, take a moment to evaluate your closet itself, including organization and storage.

1. **Your wardrobe should be clean and organized.** No piles on the floor, no wads in the corner. Do what you can to keep everything tidy, as it will keep your clothes in wearable shape for longer.

2. **Make sure your clothing, shoes, and accessories are visible and safely stored.** Again, you won't wear what you can't see. Do your best to create a wardrobe space with few hidden corners.

3. **Eyeball your available storage for future purchases.** You will, eventually, go shopping. Do you have room for any new items? If not, can you reconfigure your current storage?

Now feel free to collapse into an exhausted heap. You've earned it.

Once you feel sufficiently recovered and revived, we'll start exploring the basics of figure flattery. Don't worry! I'll be there. I won't let anyone cinch your waist or stick you in a pair of platform wedges without your consent.

BEFRIEND YOUR TAILOR

Many women despair of shopping because nothing seems to fit perfectly off the rack. This is because manufacturers are unable to churn out garments in the variety of shapes and sizes that Mother Nature creates within the actual human population. It can feel aggravating to bring freshly bought garments to the tailor, but the payoff will be a wardrobe of clothing that feels good, looks good, and fits your unique frame perfectly.

If you're about to buy a garment that needs tailoring:
- Ask store employees if alternate sizes are available. Many stores stock petite and tall sizes, and some offer styles designed to work with curvy figures.
- Ask store employees if complimentary alterations are available. Don't be shy!
- Assuming both of those options fail, leave the price tags on and keep your receipt. Take the item to your tailor and get a price quote. If it's worth the extra money to make the garment fit, clip the tags and dive in. If not, return it.

If you think everything in your closet may need tailoring:
- Request help from a personal shopper at a department store. Perhaps you aren't aware of speciality sizing and fit options.
- Consider learning to do simple alterations, like hemming, yourself.
- Take garments in waves. Bring a few key items per trip, pay for them, and reincorporate them into your wardrobe. Repeat when you've got the money.

Remember:
- Tailors can add sleeves, shorten sleeves, or alter sleeve styles.
- Garments can be made shorter and smaller, but depending on seam allowances, some can also be made longer and larger. Ask!
- Skilled tailors can repair rips, stains, and damage. If you can't imagine how you'd fix a garment yourself, take it to the pros.
- A good tailor can tear apart and rebuild just about any garment. It can be incredibly costly, but in some cases it's worth the dough.

Gracey, Fashion for Giants
fashionforgiants.blogspot.com

Chapter 3: Learning to Flatter Your Figure

TOOLS YOU'LL NEED:
Style Journal

Now that you've spent some time defining your current style—identifying your personal icons, writing about your dressing preferences, and building some preliminary outfits—you're primed and ready to learn about figure flattery. Before you can consider adding any new garments, you need to know which styles work with your fabulous figure and which ones fight it.

Understanding figure-flattery is vital to the creation of a lasting, personalized style. When you're exhausted, crabby, or sore, "unconfining" becomes the order of the day, and you feel compelled to throw on a tunic the size of a circus tent. But hopefully those days are relatively rare. Because overall, clothing that fits your body and accentuates your favorite features *should* make you feel serene and goddess-like. So most days you should reach for garments that do just that.

But what, exactly, makes a garment flattering?

Well, for starters:

• **Flattering clothing lies flat against your body.** If you've got a bubble of dress material perched atop your butt, a shoulder seam that creeps toward your neck, or a side-entry pant pocket that wings out, you're wearing something that neither fits nor flatters your specific shape. Seek styles and sizes that sit flat and quiet against you, even when you are in motion.

• **Flattering clothing doesn't pull, pinch, or subdivide.** If there are five deep, giant wrinkles that extend from the fly of your slacks to your hipbones, those slacks are too tight.* If cap sleeves dig into your upper arms, seek a different sleeve style. If your skirt's waistband causes your midsection to spill out over its top, go up a size. Don't have a meltdown. That skirt size is just an arbitrary number, and you can cut the tag right out if it rankles you. Your clothing should caress your body, not squeeze it.

• **Flattering clothing works with your eyes, hair, and skin tone.** There are entire books on this subject, but here's the cheat-sheet:

Clothing that fits properly will glide over your body. It will never pull, pinch, or subdivide.

Keri, Headlines & Hemlines
headlinesandhemlines.com

* I mean *deep* and *giant*. All pants pull a little bit across the pelvis, no matter the style and no matter the wearer. But theres a difference between mild creasing and enormous, highly visible wrinkles.

Hold a solid block of color next to your gorgeous visage. Wrap it all the way around your face with a thatch of your hair peeking out. Look in a mirror in a well-lit room and ask yourself these questions: Does it brighten or dull your eye color? How does it play off your hair color? Do you look healthy and robust, or wan and sickly?

Select clothing that helps you create your desired silhouette.

Lisa, Respect the Shoes
respecttheshoes.blogspot.com

• **Flattering clothing creates a silhouette that pleases your eye.** Please note that I did *not* say "flattering clothing makes you look skinny, busty, tall, and hipless." If those are your goals, that's completely fine. But if you'd rather show off your shapely bum or minimize your bust, by all means do so. And trust yourself to know when clothing is contributing to your preferred silhouette. When you throw on a sweater that hugs in all the wrong places, you peel it off immediately, don't you? When you squeeze into a dress that makes you think your waist looks teeny but your calves look like sequoias, you know something is amiss. And when you pull on a pair of jeans that balances your hips, hugs your thighs, or shows off your shapely calves, you know you've found a winner. You already know your own best silhouette, so seek garments that present that silhouette to the observing world.

I realize that last mandate may seem daunting. Instinct is a great place to start, and you know on sight when something is eye-searingly horrendous on you. But it's not all gut reaction. Training your eye to identify flattering styles takes time and practice.

But it also takes an intimate knowledge of your figure. Understanding your body's unique shape is essential to locating clothing that will flatter your shape, and flattering clothing will help you cultivate your ideal style. Familiarizing yourself with the intricacies of your body's shape can feel like a tall order, but it's well worth the investment of time and energy to puzzle it out. Read on for some simple steps you can take to acquaint yourself with your figure and its needs.

FIGURING OUT YOUR FIGURE

The shortcut to understanding your body is to identify your body type, yet pinpointing your body type can seem impossible. You pore over photographs of women in black unitards labeled as "pears," "apples," and "string beans," and see nary a one that resembles your own body. (Shortly after that, you ardently wish that the female form could be described in non-food terms.) I've seen body-type breakdowns with as many as twelve possible options and never once found an example body shaped like my own.

And I know why.

Because almost no one is a true pear, apple, or string bean. Most of us are string beans with bulky, muscular thighs, or pears with relatively broad shoulders, or some variation on the template that makes fruit-specific clothing styles look atrocious on our actual bodies. And while body-type breakdowns are meant to serve as guidelines, the folks who write them never seem to offer work-arounds for those of us with variations on the highlighted themes.

Nevertheless, you'll have a hell of a time finding clothing that flatters your form if you don't familiarize yourself with your form. You need to know about your shape and proportions to effectively evaluate clothes—both new and old—and to know they conform to the four figure-flattery mandates listed above. But you needn't base that familiarization on body type. Why use such a confining and imperfect system? I've got a better, simpler, and more personalized way to learn about your marvelously unique shape. So grab your style journal, haul out the full-length mirror, strip down to your undies, and take a long, hard look.

What aspects jump out as your defining physical traits? Look at yourself in the mirror and identify which bits are markedly large, small, or relatively out of proportion. Try not to judge yourself and don't use someone else's body as a point of comparison. Just take an honest look. Do you have a prominent stomach, long neck, tiny feet? Do your arms seem short, your

shoulders broad, your breasts small? Does your torso seem much longer than your legs, or vice versa? Look at everything, not just the major regions like hips, midsection, and bust. Examine your wrists and ankles, leg and arm length, calf and thigh circumference. Then jot down some notes in your Style Journal about the features of your physical form that seem to define it.

Let's use me as an example. I have broad shoulders, which make my A-and-a-half-cup breasts seem relatively small. My hips and thighs are full, which make my natural waist seem bitsy. My feet are well proportioned to my muscular calves, but my hands and wrists are small compared to my arms.

Notice how I am noting my features mainly in comparison to my other features. What's the point in comparing my boobs to Salma Hayek's? Even if I had her boobs, I wouldn't have her stature, her shoulder span, or any other aspect of her figure. Her boobs would look totally different on my frame. I'd rather focus on how *my* boobs interact with other aspects of *my* frame.

What do you love best about your body? Every woman secretly longs to brag about her flat abs, ladylike collarbone, long legs, or shapely derrière. Subtler physical traits can become favorites, too: radiant skin, lustrous hair, delicate bone structure.

Put your clothes back on and sit down with your trusty Style Journal. List your top ten favorite physical aspects, right off the top of your head. Now rank them from the thing you love most to the thing you love least. Think about why you adore these traits so much. Did you inherit them from beloved relatives? Work hard for them on your own? Do they set you apart from the crowd? Think about clothes you already own that accentuate these features and write down any techniques you already employ to draw attention to them. Think about how you feel when you're able to show off your body's best and how differently you'd feel if doing so were an everyday priority.

Attempting to identify yourself within a set of predetermined figure types is often frustrating and confusing. Your body is unique and wedging it into some arbitrary category can feel downright unnatural. But these two simple steps are both personalized and detailed, helping you identify traits that define your body and features that make it marvelous. Thinking long and hard about these two questions will give you a good idea of what you've got, so that you can decide how to work with what you've got.

Now you have a clear idea of how your body looks. How are you going to flatter it?

PRIORITIES, PRIORITIES

Having gathered some basic information about how your body is shaped and proportioned, now give some preliminary thought to your figure-flattery priorities. What about your body should be in the spotlight at all times, no matter what you're wearing? What about your body would you rather disguise, if anything? Based on what you now know about your defining traits and favorite physical aspects, how do you want your body to appear to the observing world?

As you mull over what you want to celebrate and what you want to diminish, consider these possible priorities:

1. **Balance.** As a teen, I avoided shoes that made my feet look small. My hips have always been relatively broad and slipping on footwear that minimized my feet just made me feel like a human bowling pin. I preferred to balance my hips with giant, clodhopper shoes. I've refined my techniques a bit since then, of course, but creating balance within my figure remains a priority for me. If the bulk of your body rests in one area, such as your chest, midsection, or butt, creating balance may be a priority for you.

2. **Minimization.** Some large-breasted women wish to minimize their chests,

Clothing can be used to create visual balance in your natural figure.

Déjà Pseu
Une Femme d'un Certain Age
unefemme.net

and some women with pronounced backsides long to disguise them. We've all got bits we want to show off, but many of us have bits we'd like to downplay, too. If you have one aspect of your figure that is considerably larger or more noticeable than the rest of your figure might dictate, minimization may be a priority for you.

3. **Maximization.** On the flip side, narrow-shouldered women often wish to enhance or artificially bulk up their frames, and some small-breasted women prefer to pad. If you have one aspect of your figure that is considerably smaller than the rest of your figure might dictate, maximization may be a priority for you.

4. **Elongation or shortening.** Legs, torsos, and arms all come in a variety of lengths—although retailers remain in denial about this—and some configurations may strike your eye as imbalanced. In extreme cases, length issues may cause fit issues. Long-legged femmes struggle to find skirts that aren't scandalously short, short legs beneath a long torso may make pants impossible to fit, and short arms on an average frame could make sleeves appear humorously long. Even those who can wear off-the-rack clothing often wish to visually adjust their proportions. If limb or midsection length cause fitting woes or visual disproportionateness, elongation or shortening may be a priority for you.

5. **Love.** Put aside all the shape, size, and balance stuff for a moment. When you completed the in-your-undies evaluation of your figure, what did you decide you absolutely adored about your bod? Prioritize highlighting your favorite features!

Many women want to create a balanced, hourglass figure, but that is not the only option. If you love your tall, rectangular frame and don't care to carve out a waistline, or you adore your ample boot-ay and feel no desire to balance it out with volume on top, never let anyone say you nay. You're defining your ideal style. *You* get to decide what to highlight and what to downplay. In fact, *you* get to decide whether or not you want to monkey with your natural proportions at all.

But should you choose to monkey, you'll need some tools to make those figure-flattery priorities into figure-flattery realities.

STYLE JOURNAL SIDE NOTE: ORGANIZATION

Very soon, your Style Journal will start to bulk up. You'll take copious notes and answer lots of important questions about your style preferences and dreams. If organization is second nature to you, you'll undoubtedly find you own ways to keep your journal in legible, accessible, comprehensible shape. But if you're already worried that your Style Journal will become a mass of scribbles, here are a few pointers:

- **Create sections.** To help you process the information you're generating, it may help to create and title sections within your Style Journal. The easiest way to do this is to copy the chapter and subsection titles right from this book. So, for instance, your Chapter 2 work would get the overall heading of "Defining My Current Style," and have subsections titled, "words that describe my current style," "questions that will help define my current style," "current most worn items," etc.

- **Write out questions.** If you just jot down answers, your efforts may become garbled and meaningless when you revisit them. Take the extra time to transcribe complete questions and *then* write your answers.

- **Include visuals.** Drawings and photos will enhance your Style Journal, so I highly recommend leaving space for them. You'll jog your memory faster and call up ideas more effectively if you've got a few visuals.

Anything you do to organize your Style Journal will help you in the future. This journal will become an important reference tool, so keep it in good shape!

Stacy, Stacyverb
stacyverb.typepad.com

Chapter 4: Building Your Figure-flattery Arsenal

TOOLS YOU'LL NEED:
Style Journal

You've got your defining physical traits and top ten favorite physical aspects in hand, and you've identified your general flattery priorities. Now it's time to dig into the specifics. How, exactly, will you minimize your hips and elongate your arms? What garments will help you emphasize your shoulders and downplay your bust?

Since we're *not* focused on fruity body types, and we're *not* insisting that you do everything in your power to create an artificial hourglass, we're gonna approach this a la carte.

In this chapter you'll find figure-flattery tips based on various body parts. Each section will offer garment and styling suggestions that will either downplay or highlight an aspect of your figure. Mix and match depending on your body shape and your figure priorities as well as your environment, peer group, activities, and even mood. Because who says you have to dress the same way every day?

As you read these suggestions, make a note in your Style Journal if any seem particularly appealing and applicable. Don't panic if you have multiple or conflicting physical traits that you want to downplay or emphasize. It's true that certain garments and styles will achieve one goal while defeating another, and you'll have to prioritize. But for now, simply compile a list of figure-flattery methods that you'd like to explore. You'll spend time experimenting with them later on and can edit your list when you do.

Now ask yourself once more: How do I want my body to appear to the observing world? Which aspects of my physical self do I want to minimize and which ones do I want to maximize in order to feel fantastic about my figure? What do I love most about my body, and how can I show it off every single day?

An eye-catching belt draws the eye down the torso and away from the neck.

Kirsten, Barking Dog Shoes
barkingdogshoes.com

NECK

Downplay

- **Scarves.** The easiest way to disguise your neck is to cover it up! Explore various materials, weights, and shapes. Test multiple knotting and tying techniques until you find one that works for you.
- **Long necklaces.** A necklace that ends low on the body—ribcage or navel instead of bust or chin—will draw the eye naturally downward and away from the neck.
- **Eye-catching belts.** If you're all in gray but sporting a bright red belt, no one will give a moment's thought to your neck. It'll be all about your waistline.
- **Deep V necklines.** Another great distraction technique is to draw attention to the bust. A plunging neckline does just that.

<u>Highlight</u>

- **Scarves.** Oh yes, indeed, scarves can be used to highlight a shapely neck as well! Pick something small and tie a square knot to the side, or create a loose cowl from a longer scarf to highlight your neck and collarbone.
- **Short necklaces.** Think of styles that sit just shy of choker placement. This style is deeply unflattering on many, but if you love the look and adore your neck, there's hardly a better way to accentuate it.
- **Crew necklines.** Since everything from clavicle downward is covered up, this face- framing style shows off a lovely neck.
- **Short hairstyles.** Although many cuts can contribute, anything in the pixie family is ideal for displaying a gorgeous neck.

Short necklaces draw the observing eye up toward the neck.

Cynthia, Addicted 2 Etsy
addicted2etsy.com

SHOULDERS

<u>Downplay</u>

- **Full skirts (for broad shoulders).** The volume on your bottom half will balance out broad shoulders quite tidily.
- **Detailed sleeves (for narrow shoulders).** Anything with a bit of a poof, stiffness or blazer-like structure, or even light padding in the shoulders, will artificially broaden narrow shoulders.

- **Belted looks.** If you have broad shoulders, belting will attract attention to your midsection and create a faux hourglass. If you have narrow shoulders, belting can do the same so long as your natural waist is at least a bit smaller than your shoulder span.
- **Deep V necklines.** Again, if the eye goes to décolletage, it won't even register shoulder width, be it broad or narrow. Boobs are way more interesting.

Highlight

- **Cap sleeves.** Since they're just a tiny distance from the shoulder itself, these sleeves serve to focus attention to your arms and shoulders.
- **Strapless tops and dresses.** Well, obviously. If shoulders are on display entirely unencumbered by straps, they'll be the focus of attention.
- **Boat necklines.** This long, narrow style creates a horizontal line across your collarbone, which ends at your shoulder's edge.
- **Racerbacks.** Since the straps on this style of tank top fall closer to the neck than thoseof a traditional tank, they make shoulders appear broad and muscular. (Hence their popularity with the weightlifting crowd.)
- **One-shouldered tops and dresses.** Even a single displayed shoulder will grab attention.

Cap sleeves will help highlight shapely shoulders.

Gracey, Fashion for Giants
fashionforgiants.blogspot.com

BUST

<u>Downplay</u>

- **Scoop necklines.** The observing eye is drawn toward exposed skin, and a scoop does this without being overly revealing. Choose an option that falls above your cleavage line.
- **Square necklines.** Same principle as a scoop style.
- **Cap sleeves.** Since this style of sleeve falls higher than the bustline, it will draw attention away from the bust. Remember that it'll make shoulders appear wider, too.
- **Large, busy prints.** A loud, colorful, large print will keep the eye occupied and draw attention away from bust proportions.
- **Large necklaces.** Big, bold necklaces draw attention away from the bust, and direct it toward your face and neck. Make sure to pick a style that ends above the bustline to avoid draping and bounce.

<u>Highlight</u>

- **Pendant necklaces.** Anything that dangles down between the girls will grab attention!
- **Deep V necklines.** The eye will fall where that V ends, so this neckline is a classic attention-grabber.
- **Boat necklines.** In addition to creating a broad shoulder line, this style accentuates and enhances the bustline if your waist is smaller than your ribcage.

Use a plunging neckline to show off a beautiful bust.

LuAnne, Weesha's World
weeshasworld.com

- **Sweetheart necklines.** This fashion-y little frame for breasts makes big ones look marvelous and small ones look larger. Magical, I tell ya.
- **Cowl necklines.** Draped fabric laid atop even the smallest bust creates the illusion of an ample bosom.
- **Ruching.** In the neckline or under the bust, this subtle gathering adds bulk to boobage.
- **Detailed or frilly necklines.** When the focus is kept up top, the bustline gets rolled into the package deal.
- **High waistlines.** If your bottom half appears to end just below your bust, that bust will be naturally highlighted. This works best when there's a good bit of contrast between the top and bottom.

ARMS

Downplay

- **Three-quarter sleeves.** The classic choice for keeping arms covered and prying eyes away. For those concerned about large arms, the sleeve ends in the typically slim forearm area, focusing attention there. For those concerned about slender arms, the sleeve covers the arm nearly to the wrist, creating a modest look.
- **Kimono-style garments.** If your concern is masking bulk in your arms, a loose and boxy sleeve style can come to the rescue. The sheer size of the sleeve can make arms appear slim in comparison. Kimono styling often works best when it involves some waist definition to balance sleeve volume.

Three-quarter sleeves flatter both full and slender arms. Cuffing or scrunching sleeves works similarly.

Rebecca, Minnchic
minnchic.com

- **Batwing sleeves.** Same principle as kimono-style garments.
- **Shawls.** For days when sleeves are undesirable but you're still feeling self-conscious about your arms, simply drape a large scarf or shawl around your shoulders and upper arms. Chic and covered!
- **Drapey sleeves.** Constricting sleeves draw the wrong kind of attention to this body part, whereas a loose, draped sleeve is unconfining, stylish, and disguises arms beautifully. Pick something that's elbow-length or longer.
- **Single-strand bracelets.** A relatively close-fitting chain or bead bracelet that hits at thewrist will draw attention toward the hand and away from the rest of the arm.

Show the world those fabulous arms in a sleeveless or halter style top or dress.

Keri, Headlines & Hemlines
headlinesandhemlines.com

Highlight

- **Sleeveless tops and dresses.** Bring on the tank tops and spaghetti straps if you want to show off your marvelous arms.
- **Cap sleeves.** The smallest sleeve available, it allows almost the entire length of the arm to be exposed and enjoyed.
- **Bangles.** Small delicate bracelets worn at the wrist can distract from upper arms, but funky chunky bangles are all about drawing attention to this lovely body part.
- **Racerbacks and halters.** Straps that fall close to the neck mean that shoulders and arms are at near-maximum exposure.
- **Strapless tops and dresses.** Shoulders and arms are both showcased when this style is worn.

MIDSECTION

<u>Downplay</u>

- **Tunics worn with slim pants.** A long top worn over slim-fitting jeans, pants, or leggings will draw focus to your legs and away from your tum.
- **Large necklaces.** Draw the eye up towards your face to keep it away from your midsection.
- **Busy prints.** If it's lumps and bumps you wish to disguise, a vibrant print will distract the observing eye.
- **Heavy knits.** Fine gauge knits can be clingy and revealing, but heavier ones have heft and drape that will do wonders to mask a midsection. Careful not to go *too* bulky, though, or you may add unwanted, excess volume.
- **Bright shoes.** Just as a necklace creates focus up top, bright, eye-catching shoes will draw the eye straight down and away from your midsection.

<u>Highlight</u>

- **Belts.** Contrasting colors, detailed, or patterned belts are ideal for attracting attention waist-ward. If you don't know how or where to belt, experiment with a scarf. Try rolling it tight to a one-inch width, slightly looser to a two-inch width, and finally a three-inch width to discover how wide your belts should be. And experiment with placement by belting under your bust, at your natural waist, and at your hips.
- **Full skirts.** Anything that nips in at the waist and then flares dramatically out will make the waist seem teensy. It's the contrast that does it!

Belts and full skirts are both fabulous tools for highlighting the midsection.

Lisa, Respect the Shoes
respecttheshoes.blogspot.com

52

- **Princess seams.** Curved seams that swoop in near the waistline cause the eye to follow their path.
- **High-waisted bottoms.** Many skirts and pants fall just below the natural waist, but styles with higher rises are more effective at highlighting the waistline. For added emphasis and interest, add a belt.
- **Contrasting colors.** The eye naturally gravitates toward contrast, so pairing a white top and black skirt, or vice versa, will make the place where those garments meet a point of interest. It's a bit like beltless belting.
- **Cuffed sleeves.** When you stand with your arms at your sides, scrunched and cuffed sleeves will end right at your natural waist. This subtly draws the eye to the narrowest part of your torso.

High-contrast tops and bottoms will draw the eye to the spot where they meet, right at the waist.

Patty, The Snug Bug
pattythesnugbug.com

HIPS

<u>Downplay</u>

- **A-line skirts and dresses.** Shapes that skim without clinging are key to distracting from hips. A-lines start small at the waist but quickly increase in width to create an "A" shape out of your lower half. Hips are totally masked, and only your shapely gams show beneath the skirt hem.

- **Full skirts.** These voluminous styles are small at the natural waist, poufy below, and completely obscure hip size and shape. This style is trickier than A-lines, though, especially for women with large busts, short torsos, or high hips.
- **Boat necklines.** Balance out hips with a broad, wide slash neckline up top.
- **Empire-waist dresses.** Some fashion experts claim these garments are a cure-all, but that is patently untrue. High-waisted dresses can be *incredibly* unflattering, so chose construction details carefully. Avoid gathers, pleats, and ruffles at the waistline. Look for designs with flat, thin waists and/or constructed from relatively heavy material with decent drape. These will raise your waistline up while disguising hips entirely.
- **Bootleg or flare pants.** It's been said a bajillion times, but it's absolutely true. A hint of volume at the ankle balances volume at the hips. Be sure to select a style that tapers at the knee before flaring out. This feature is key to visually defining your leg shape.

Bootcut jeans are a classic choice for downplaying hips since the slight hem flare creates balance.

Déjà Pseu
Une Femme d'un Certain Age
unefemme.net

Highlight

- **Skinny jeans and pants.** Although these styles put your entire lower half on display, hips are often a focal point, as that's where pockets and detailing reside. Wear a shirt that hits at the hipbone or higher for optimum hip flaunting.

- **Miniskirts.** Not just for gam showcasing, miniskirts do a great job of highlighting hips. Since hips and upper thighs are all that's covered, this area of the body becomes a focal point.
- **Hip-slung belts.** The name says it all! This style—worn over a skirt or pair of jeans—draws the eye hip-ward.
- **Hip-length tunics and tops.** As mentioned above, the eye naturally gravitates toward contrast. If you want your hips seen, wear a top that ends right at hip level and a bottom in a noticeably different color, texture, or finish.
- **Pencil skirts.** A skirt that nips in at the waist and again at the knees is pretty much designed with hips in mind.

STYLE JOURNAL SIDE NOTE: DUPLICATION

I've mentioned this before, but it bears repeating: write down questions, phrases, and key concepts into your Style Journal. It may seem like make-work, but it's not. The act of writing something in longhand can crystallize ideas and insights.

In all chapters, but especially in this one, **consider copying down questions, responses, and ideas that seem relevant.** For instance, as you move through the detailed lists of figure-flattery options, jot down the ones you currently use and the ones you're interested in trying. Write the name of the relevant body part, the applicable technique, and why it works. Also note if you believe that a certain tip will achieve one goal while simultaneously defeating another. Consider writing down the four elements of figure flattering clothing so you can commit them to memory, or refer to your journal for reminders on future shopping excursions.

Collecting all of these details in your Style Journal will make it more comprehensive and useful when you consult it in the future.

BUTT

<u>Downplay</u>

- **Bootleg or flare pants.** If you want to completely hide your butt, go for a skirt or dress instead. But if minimization is all you seek, the balancing properties of pants with a slightly flared hem can work wonders.

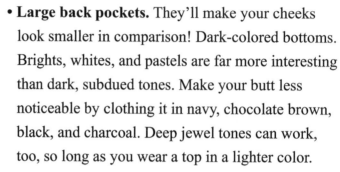

If you want to highlight your derrière, skinny jeans or pants worn with a butt-grazing shirt will do the trick.

Gracey, Fashion for Giants
fashionforgiants.blogspot.com

- **Large back pockets.** They'll make your cheeks look smaller in comparison! Dark-colored bottoms. Brights, whites, and pastels are far more interesting than dark, subdued tones. Make your butt less noticeable by clothing it in navy, chocolate brown, black, and charcoal. Deep jewel tones can work, too, so long as you wear a top in a lighter color.
- **Square and boat necklines.** Both styles create some volume up top without adding bulk, balancing a prominent butt from above.
- **A-line skirts and dresses.** Full skirts can make a high or full butt look even higher or fuller, so stick to the less extreme A-line. The cloth should glide over hips and butt and that the zippers shouldn't bunch in the lower back. Also make sure your hems stay even; depending on your shape, skirts may sit higher in back than front.

<u>Highlight</u>

- **Skinny jeans and pants.** Formfitting pants are fantastic for highlighting the derrière. Try ponte knit or a fabric with stretch.

56

- **Cropped jackets.** Since this style sits high on the body, the butt remains exposed. Wear a form-fitting skirt or pants to complete the backside-centric look.
- **Small back pockets.** They'll make your cheeks look larger in comparison!
- **Contoured seaming.** If there are stitches and contoured panels gracing your backside, they'll draw attention to its curves.
- **Pencil skirts.** Wear a shorter top to give this style optimum bum-enhancing capabilities.

THIGHS

<u>Downplay</u>

- **Long tunics.** Pair leggings (yes, leggings!) with a loose tunic that hits just above the knee. Thighs are hidden, calves accentuated.
- **A-line and full skirts.** Can you tell I adore these pieces for anything lower bod-minimization related? They really are magical critters. For thigh disguise, pick a knee-length style. These nipped-waist skirts become quickly voluminous below the belt and will keep thighs a mystery while letting calves do all the legwork.
- **Wide-leg pants.** Any pant style that tapers will draw attention to the circumference difference between thigh and calf. A wide leg conceals all.

Leggings, when worn with a long tunic, can flatter many leg sizes and shapes. The tunic itself helps to downplay the thighs.

Kirsten, Barking Dog Shoes
barkingdogshoes.com

- **Dark bottoms, bright tops.** Subdued shades on your lower half will downplay, while vibrant hues up top distract. (Add an accessory or incorporate a pattern to tie your two halves together.)
- **Floor-length, flared skirts.** Essentially wide-legs in skirt format, these skirts keep thighs under wraps. Pick heavier materials like twill or ponte and styles with gores for shaping.

Highlight

- **Short shorts.** If you've got the gams and you've got the gumption, these summer favorites will show the world the whole length of your legs.
- **Miniskirts and minidresses.** Same principle as short-shorts. A high hemline means highlighted thighs.
- **Distressed jeans.** Torn bits and exposed threads on the upper leg will focus attention on your thighs.
- **Border prints on knee-length skirts.** A dress or skirt with a printed border at the hem will draw attention thigh-ward.

CALVES

Downplay

- **Low-vamp shoes.** To make calves look narrower, show as much of the top portion of your foot as you can. You want to make your calf appear as long as possible.

The high hemlines on miniskirts and minidresses will serve to highlight the thighs.

LuAnne, Weesha's World
weeshasworld.com

- **Slacks.** Any non-skinny style of pant can both disguise and minimize. Whether your calves are large or small, sticking to long pants and avoiding short skirts is the most effective way of drawing attention away from them.
- **Patterned tights.** If you are going the skirt route, a pair of tights with a busy pattern can become your best friend. The eye will be so concerned with the design that it'll register less information about calf size or shape. Caveat: avoid horizontal stripes if attempting to slenderize your calves.
- **A-line skirts.** Pick a skirt that hits at the knee or a smidge higher. The flared shape adds volume *above* the calf, making your lower leg appear smaller.
- **Floor-length, flared skirts.** These work for the total hide. If it's calves alone you're hoping to downplay, try to pair these skirts with a formfitting top to balance the volume.
- **Ankle-length leggings.** Paired with tunics and dresses, these can be just darling. Choose dark colors to minimize impact and wear with heels to elongate the calf itself.

Just about any pant or jean with non-skinny leg openings will help to downplay the calves.

Fabienne, The House in the Clouds
thehouseintheclouds.com

Highlight

- **Cropped pants.** A crop that hits a few inches below the knee does an amazing job of showing off shapely calves. Slim-fitting crops generally appear more contemporary than wide ones.

- **Mid-calf skirts and dresses.** If you want to draw attention to your calves, placing a hemline right across them works wonders. This is particularly effective for women who wish to visually widen narrow calves, as mid-calf hems do just that.

- **Knee-length skirts and dresses.** If you'd rather show off everything from the knee down, a slightly shorter hemline does the trick!

- **Ankle-strap shoes and booties.** Since both styles end at the high ankle, they attract attention to the nearby calf.

- **Nude shoes.** Renowned for their leg-elongating properties, shoes that match your skin tone will also highlight your calves. Wear them with dresses and skirts for the highest impact.

ELONGATION

<u>Arms</u>

- **Cap sleeves.** These diminutive sleeves make the arm seem miles long in comparison.

- **Wide-strap tops and dresses.** A broad strap works better than a spaghetti strap, as all attention is focused on the arm and less so on the clavicle.

- **Belting at the natural waist or higher.** This technique can make arms appear longer, as it shifts the overall silhouette upward.

Booties or short boots that end
at the ankle or just above
will draw attention to the calves.

Stacy, Stacyverb
stacyverb.typepad.com

Dresses with dropwaist detailing will visually elongate the torso.

Audi, Fashion for Nerds
geekthreads.blogspot.com

Torso

- **Low-rise pants.** Moving the waistline artificially downward elongates the torso.
- **Dropwaist dresses.** Bringing the waistline down to hip level creates the illusion of torso length.
- **Hip-slung belts.** Making the hips a focal point adds length to the silhouette.

Legs

- **Nude shoes.** Skin-tone shoes make legs appear longer as the give the eye no resting place until it hits the ground.
- **Above-the-knee skirts and shorts.** Anything with a short hemline will make legs seem lengthy in comparison.
- **High waists.** Pulling the eye up higher than your natural waist gives the impression of super long gams, even with a longer hemline. If the observer thinks your waist is up near your armpits, the assumption is that your legs start just below your armpits.

SHORTENING

Arms

- **Half sleeves.** A sleeve that chops the arm in half at the elbow will naturally shorten it.
- **Low-rise bottoms.** If your waistline is artificially lowered, arms seem shorter in comparison.
- **Cuff bracelets.** Obscuring the wrist has the net effect of making forearms seem shorter, which can shorten the entire arm, too.

Belting high or opting for garments with high waistlines will visually shorten the torso.

Cynthia, Addicted 2 Etsy
addicted2etsy.com

Torso

- **High waistlines.** Creating an artificially high waist effectively shortens a long torso.
- **Cropped jackets and sweaters.** Worn over a contrasting top or dress, these "shorties" have the same effect as high waistlines. The eye stops where the jacket ends, which is higher than the true waist of a gal with a long torso.
- **Detailed necklines.** Drawing the eye toward the bust and face keeps the focus high on the body.
- **Leg elongation.** See above tips. The longer the legs look, the more balanced the torso appears.

Legs

- **Flat shoes.** Heels elongate, flats shorten. For optimum shortening, choose a flat shoe that hits at the ankle, like a gladiator sandal or bootie.
- **Cropped pants.** Bottoms that either show or obscure the entire leg will lengthen it. A pant that stops somewhere in the calf region can make legs appear artificially short.
- **Calf-height boots.** Not only do these boots make calves appear wider, but also by cutting the calf in half, they serve to shorten the entire leg.

Is this list complete? Heck no. This is your starter arsenal. Once you start playing around with some of these minimization and accentuation techniques, you'll begin to learn more about your proportions, your assets, and how to create beautiful bodily balance.

Speaking of which, take some time to play now. After you've identified which of these techniques interest you based on your personal figure-flattery priorities, put them to the test in real life. Find items in your wardrobe that should, in theory, downplay/highlight a certain aspect of your figure. Try them on and see what you think. If you don't own any high-waisted pants but are dying to see if they really will accentuate your waistline, track down a pair at your friendly neighborhood department store and snap a few dressing room photos for future reference. Does the specified garment have the desired effect on *your* body? If not, try a few of the other recommended solutions. Then go back to the list of potential options you made in your journal, and note which ones truly do work their magic for you.

As I mentioned at the beginning of this chapter, some of these tricks will achieve one goal while simultaneously defeating another. Sometimes it's possible to employ multiple figure-flattery strategies at a time; sometimes it's not. As you play, hone in on the styles and garments that work best for you holistically, flattering desirable aspects without drawing attention to less-beloved ones. These will become your figure flattery bread and butter. Techniques that further one goal while hindering another should be used sparingly and only in situations that won't make you fret over whatever trait is being revealed or highlighted. Make note of these double-edged figure-flattery techniques in your Style Journal, too.

By now your journal should be filling up with valuable insights about your body shape and stylistic preferences. You've got a whole lotta theory under your belt right now, and I'm sure you're dying to put it into practice. At the mall. This instant.

But instead, let's apply it to what you already own, to see what *else* you can learn about yourself and your style.

Dressing can be fun. Really!

Lisa, Respect the Shoes
respecttheshoes.blogspot.com

GREAT LENGTHS

In my experience, virtually nothing style-related is universal. But having worked with dozens of makeover clients, I've found that confusion over garment length is absolutely rampant. There is flexibility here, of course, but in the interest of clarifying what seems to be an epidemic of misunderstanding:

You need different lengths of shirts in your arsenal. A shirt worn with a skirt should be shorter—about one hand's width below your navel. A shirt worn with pants should be longer—about one hand's width above your crotch point. Adjust as needed if dressing to correct torso length, but if your torso is relatively balanced, keep these guidelines in mind.

Lisa, Respect the Shoes
respecttheshoes.blogspot.com

Rebecca, Minnchic
minnchic.com

You need different lengths of pants in your arsenal. Ideally, you should have pants hemmed for heels and pants hemmed for flats. Your pants should be one-half inch to three-quarters of an inch above the ground regardless of footwear, and that means flats-pants will be far too short for heels, and heels-pants will be far too long for flats.

Gracey, Fashion for Giants
fashionforgiants.blogspot.com

Skirt hemlines affect your proportions. If you're petite, a calf-length skirt will shorten your legs and overall silhouette. If you have incredibly long legs, wearing a miniskirt may make you appear to be *all* legs. When considering a skirt choice, give some thought to how it impacts your proportions.

This does *not* mean you must purchase everything in two or more lengths or styles. It means that you cannot wear all of your pants with all of your shoes. It means that certain tops will suit skirts better than pants. It may limit your combinations, but it does not limit your overall dressing versatility.

Cynthia, Addicted 2 Etsy
addicted2etsy.com

Chapter 5: Refining Your Ideal Style

TOOLS YOU'LL NEED:
Style Journal

Before you can decide who you want to be, you must understand who you are today. Having worked through the previous chapters, you should know yourself pretty darned well, stylistically speaking. You've explored your current style, identified your defining physical traits, and considered how best to flatter your figure. Now that you understand your style as it stands today, you're ready to start sketching out the style of your dreams.

If someone asked you to describe your ideal style, how would you respond? In this tantalizing hypothetical, you have no financial constraints, endless closet space, and every available manufactured item at your easy disposal. Given these extremely loose parameters, most women latch onto one of two extremes: celebrity fantasy or wholesale pragmatism.

"Everything in Sarah Jessica Parker's closet. And don't forget the shoes."

Or:

"A wardrobe full of pieces that are comfy, soft, machine-washable, stain-resistant, wrinkle-proof, and snag-proof. Oh, and they've all gotta match each other."

Raiding SJP's cupboard would be a gas, and a closet full of interchangeable washables would be dreamy. But the "ideal" I want you to focus on isn't based on straight-up object lust or total ease-of-use. What I'm envisioning is a highly personalized style that centers on your body, your tastes, and your lifestyle. Envision a set of ideas about dressing and a set of core items that reflect who you are and that present your best self to the outside world. I believe that a truly ideal style will suit your unique figure and revolve around your personal wardrobe staples.

A truly ideal style starts with you.

FOCUS, PEOPLE

Before we tackle the more concrete aspects of refining your ideal style, let's brainstorm. Try using these questions to guide your ruminations and jot down your answers in your Style Journal.

- **What is your top use priority?** Washability? Versatility? Durability? What traits do you seek in a garment or accessory?

- **What are your top three figure-flattery priorities?** Do you want to show off your calves at all times? Downplay your shoulders? Emphasize your bust? What do you want the clothing in your ideal wardrobe to do for you? Consult your Style Journal for guidance; your recent work identifying your top ten physical aspects and your experimentation with specific figure-flattery techniques should guide you.

- **What is your top comfort priority?** Do all shoes need to be worthy of an hour's walk? Do you have a sensitive midsection and need to avoid anything that squeezes? Do structured shoulders make you want to pull your hair out in large handfuls?

- **What are your color priorities?** Are you neutral-focused? Need more brights? Don't care as long as the color works with your complexion? Interested in incorporating more patterns? Which colors make you feel happiest, loveliest, most powerful?

- **How much overlap do you want between work and weekend?** If you dress differently for your job than you do for leisure, take a moment to consider *how* differently. Are you comfortable with two decidedly separate looks? Would you rather have more continuity? Are you willing to go more casual during the week or fancier on the weekend?

- **What do you want to change?** Remember the work in Chapter 2, when you wrote about your current style and mused on what you wanted to keep constant and what you wanted to change? Turn to that page in your Style Journal and take another look. Now that you've gained some figure-flattery knowledge, are those desires still as strong? Have they shifted? Knowing what you know now, what do you want to change about your style?

- **What adjectives describe your ideal style?** You've already got a list that delineates your current style, but what about your dream style? Do you want to be a minimalist, a romantic, a Bohemian? Do you want to be bold or classic? Aim for at least ten words. You'll employ them as you evaluate potential new purchases.

- **What do you want to avoid?** Is looking fresh and current a priority? Do you worry about dressing older or younger than you appear? Are there certain items or styles that carry negative associations? Make sure you know what you *don't* want as well as what you do want.

Jot it all down in your Style Journal, of course, since this information will be priceless once you start shopping.

Sadly, that time is not yet upon us. Before you can start acquiring new items, you must make sure that they'll supplement and enhance your current wardrobe. Because, believe it or not, *most* of the pillars of your ideal style already lurk in the depths of your closet. Your style staples are hanging in there, I promise. You just need to identify them.

MUST-HAVE IS A FOUR-LETTER WORD

Nearly every style guide includes a list of wardrobe staples, items that every fashionable woman simply MUST own. These garments and accessories are generally conservative, classic, and a bit dull…yet they are meant to form the foundation of every modern woman's well-rounded wardrobe.

In my experience, these must-have lists are seldom helpful in generating productive shopping lists. Sure, they're great jumping-off points if you've just graduated from college and have no idea how to transition from ripped jeans to business casual. But even then, most of those lists do not address the following issues:

- Pieces like button-front shirts and pencil skirts do not work for all body shapes.
- In this day and age, buying a quality suit *isn't* always a wise investment.
- Some of us just don't *like* pearls, dammit.

There is no one-list-fits-all set of classic items that will suit every possible body type, budget, and lifestyle. Plus, so many must-have lists overlook body diversity. They offer up items that flatter only a small segment of the female population and tell the rest of us to *just keep looking* until we find trench coats that don't make us feel like walking sacks of potatoes. And besides all that, few women could purchase a list of classic, must-have items and feel complete. These items may encompass a fashion icon's ideal style, but they seldom reflect the wants and needs of us regular gals.

So screw the sanctioned must-haves. Every wardrobe has workhorse items and staples, sodetermine yours. Who says you have to play by someone else's rules?

WHAT MAKES A STAPLE?

You may be saying to yourself, "Now, hold the phone. If I'm aiming for my ideal, shouldn't I be pushing myself to evolve instead of relying on my well-worn stylistic habits?" And I hear that. But the bald fact is that you're NOT going to change yourself all that much, even if you plan to completely overhaul your wardrobe. If you've always loved jeans, you'll still love them. You'll just seek out pairs that flatter your figure more effectively. If pastel colors make you want to puke, that is unlikely to change. So even if it turns out that you look smashing in pale pink, you'll continue to avoid pale pink when you procure new duds. Studying your current preferences and noting your long-loved favorites will help you hone your current wardrobe and choose new garments that'll have true staying power.

So, head over to your closet, grab your current wardrobe staples, and set them on your bed. Don't confine yourself to a single category. Consider garments and accessories that are dressy/work staples, casual staples, and crossover staples.

Items that qualify must be:

1. **Versatile.** True wardrobe staples will work across seasons and occasions. You may pull out that strappy sundress for every fancy summer party you attend, but those chinos that get year-round wear are better qualified for stapledom.
2. **Flattering.** For a refresher on what "flattering" means, flip back to Chapter 3. But in short, you may strip off your work clothes and throw on your stained, ripped, oversize sweatshirt every day when you arrive home, but it's no staple. That go-to V-neck sweater that does wonders for your rack? Staple it.
3. **Frequently worn.** You may *want* to include that pair of sky-high wedges as a staple, but consider how often you strap them on. Frequency will depend on the size and depth of your wardrobe, but I'd say don't consider anything you wear less than once per month a staple item.
4. **Central to your look.** Bras are not wardrobe staples, although they are versatile, flattering, and frequently worn. But if a certain brooch or tee shirt feels quintessentially "you," if anything you own truly defines and supports your current style, it's staple-worthy.

Items that don't fit all four criteria aren't wardrobe staples; make sure every piece you pull qualifies. You may come up with five items, or you may come up with thirty-five. No matter the number, gather them up and divide them into dressy/work, casual, and crossover. If you don't have an item or two in each category, go back to the closet and identify a few secondary staples. Make an entry for each in your journal and leave some room for notes.

STYLE JOURNAL SIDE NOTE: PRIORITIZATION

Your Style Journal work for this chapter forces you to pick and name some personal style priorities, which can feel daunting. Here two opposite yet equally effective tactics for tackling this work:

1. **Take notes first.** Some folks are fine with scribbles and mistakes and crossed-out words. I'm a lifelong perfectionist, so that stuff drives me insane. Since you'll be doing lots of thinking and hashing-out throughout this chapter, consider using loose paper for your rough drafts. Then, once you've drawn some solid conclusions, refine and copy them into your Style Journal.

2. **Include everything.** If, on the other hand, you prefer to use your journal as a true journal—an ever-changing tome that documents this process in its entirety—consider including everything. Write in essay form as you think about your use, color, and comfort priorities so you can see how you drew your final conclusions. Consider underlining those conclusions or using a different color of ink to give them weight and make them stand out.

Now that you've identified your central, defining items, what can they teach you about your current style? And how can they get you closer to achieving your ideal style?

LEARNING FROM THE PAST

The pillars of your current wardrobe will both inform your future purchases and influence which non-staple items stay in heavy rotation. Take some time to think and write about your staples in your Style Journal.

What do they have in common? Are they all washable, all neutral in color, all retro-influenced, all highly embellished?

What about them is flattering and why? Which of the highlighting/downplaying tips from Chapter 4 does each piece evoke? Are all of the bottoms fabulous at showing off your hips? Do all of the tops minimize your strong shoulders? Have you got some colors in there that make your skin glow and your eyes shine? (Oh, and everything lays flat, doesn't pull, works with your complexion, and creates your preferred silhouette, RIGHT?)

What about them would you change? Is there anything that irritates you about these staples? Is that blazer just a little too itchy? That blouse prone to armpit stains? If you could tweak these items, what would you change?

Are they ideal? Do these items fit the use and comfort priorities you've defined? Will they work both during the week and on the weekend? How do they figure into the parameters for your ideal style that you explored earlier in this chapter?

Now flip back to your lists from Chapter 3. Consider and note:

1. How do these staple items play off your defining physical traits?
2. Do they highlight what you love best about your body?
3. Do they align with your figure-flattery priorities?

They should, since "flattering" was criterion number two for a staple

item. But if any staple item doesn't support your priorities as previously defined, evaluate it carefully. We all have beloved items that are oversized or strangely cut, but they make up for their unflattering shapes through artistic value, added interest, or emotional significance. But those items shouldn't be staples; they should be "occasionals." If a garment snuck through this process that doesn't help you flaunt your bodacious bod, consider demoting it to non-staple status.

Look back at the notes you made about each staple and identify any overlapping traits. Synthesize these specific observations into more general ones. For instance, if your staple group includes three tops with cropped shapes to help visually shorten your long torso, write: "I like cropped tops because they shorten my long torso." If everything in all three staple piles is 100 percent cotton, silk, or linen, write: "I like natural fibers." In this way, you'll begin to formulate specific language that describes your style.

And the great thing about these general observations is that they'll both encapsulate your current style and contribute to your ideal style. These are your personal sartorial preferences, as reflected by past decisions and to be carried forward by future choices. If you like natural fibers, your current style includes them now and your ideal style will include them in the future. When you cull your wardrobe, you'll have vetted criteria upon which to base your decisions. And you can evaluate any new acquisitions on your carefully honed stylistic

preferences. Once you're able to boil down what you've learned about your personal wardrobe staples, you'll have an outline for your highly personalized, ideal style.

You already know your figure and how you want to flatter it, and you've just identified the garments and accessories that both define your current style and will inform your future style. Now you're ready to evaluate the rest of your closet.

HOW IDEAL ARE YOU?

It may be daunting to ponder transforming your current style into something more aligned with your fashion fantasies, but believe me when I tell you that the contents of your closet will make a fantastic base for your ideal wardrobe. Especially now that you are familiar with your figure-flattery priorities, have charted your ideal style parameters, and have defined a few personal staples. You've got all the skills you need to undertake the most thorough wardrobe culling *ever*, to ruthlessly ditch any items that fail to fit your personal parameters, and to come away with a set of garments that will become the foundation for your expanded style.

That's right: we've arrived at Purge Number Two.

You need to sift through everything AGAIN to weed out the lingering losers, but you also need to get the one thousand-foot view of your wardrobe. You are likely missing a handful of pieces that will make your closet feel more complete and will support the style you are gradually building, but you'll never know what's missing if you don't know what's already there. So let's examine and cull again.

1. **Determine how each item fits into your ideal style.**

   Ask yourself: Does it fit with your color, comfort, and use priorities? Does it transition easily from work to weekend? Does it reflect any of the adjectives you've used to describe your ideal style? Consult your Style Journal as needed to answer these questions. Any item that aligns with three or more of your personal style ideals should stay. Any item that only hits two marks or less should find a new home.

2. **Evaluate each item for figure flattery.**

   Clothes that work with your figure easily and naturally—based on the four tenets of garment flattery—should be kept. Clothes that align with your personal figure-flattery priorities and make you feel beautiful, powerful, and confident belong in your closet. Simple as that.

   Should you come across flattering garments that don't fit with your ideal style but still look amazing on you, think hard before you discard. You're in transition now, and it will be beneficial to have a foundation of items that make you look and feel fantastic while you continue to hone your style and your ultimate wardrobe.

   Sparingly keep clothes that don't naturally flatter you. If you love them so much it hurts, or if wearing them makes you happy despite how they fight your body, they can stay. But *don't* hang on to unflattering items just because they were expensive or gifts or fit a body you had long ago. (See Chapter 2 for a refresher on why and how to jettison clothing with negative associations.)

3. Decide which items make you feel the best.

Ditch any clothing that makes you feel awkward, unkempt, disproportionate, stodgy, sad, strange, or badly in any way *at all*. Period. Only clothing that makes you feel comfortable, serene, beautiful, and perfectly yourself should live inside your closet. Dressing is a very emotional endeavor. Make sure that all of the emotions surrounding your wardrobe are positive ones.

Hold up each item you own, ask these three questions, and decide its fate. Simple as that. Keepers go back in the closet. Everything else should be given to friends and family, donated to charity, consigned, or sold. (If I find out you've sent wearable clothes to the landfill, I will be forced to come to your home and throw a conniption fit in your living room.) Your closet may look frighteningly empty at this point, but rest in the knowledge that *everything* remaining is aligned with your priorities. And you're gonna go shopping soon. Promise. Now, get the rejects out of sight, admire your meticulously culled wardrobe, and order a celebratory pizza.

As you chow down, look back on everything you've accomplished as you worked through the past three chapters. You should be pretty darned impressed with yourself, lady. You've learned the four tenets of figure flattery, identified your defining physical traits, outlined which of those traits make you swell with pride, and researched which garments showcase your loveliness best. Then you homed in on your personal figure-flattery priorities and grabbed some dressing tips from the smorgasbord. You pinpointed your wardrobe staples and gave some thought to how their commonalities will influence your ideal style. Then you did a second pass at culling your current wardrobe, evaluating each piece for flattery and utility. That's a boatload of stylistic self-knowledge you've just accumulated. More than many women amass in an entire lifetime. And everything you've learned will influence your next steps toward building an ideal style that centers on your body, your tastes, and your lifestyle.

WORKING FOR THE WEEKEND

Many women who work day jobs maintain a work wardrobe and a completely separate weekend wardrobe. The work wardrobe typically includes clean, classic, conservative pieces that reflect personal style but are also office-appropriate. The weekend wardrobe may be somewhat congruent to the work wardrobe...but it also may be *completely* different—stocked with baggy jeans and sweatshirts; influenced by a sharply defined aesthetic, like steampunk or rockabilly; or brimming with frilly romantic, super tough, or highly whimsical pieces.

And for some, this is the only way. Work garb must conform to work rules, and if those rules are rigid and oppressive, then breaking them into tiny little bits on the weekend can be liberating. Vital, even.

But for those with a little workplace dress code leeway, I recommend merging work and weekend as much as possible. Maintaining two drastically different wardrobes can create style identity crises and forcing some of your office-ready clothes and accessories into weekend wear can heal that rift. Dressy tops paired with jeans, heels in an otherwise casual mix, and other tiny injections of formality into dressed-down looks can create an amazing bridge between workweek and weekend looks.

Consider this suggestion as you evaluate your current items and mull potential new purchases.

Rebecca, Minnchic
minnchic.com

Chapter 6: Merging Your Current and Ideal Styles

<u>TOOLS YOU'LL NEED:</u>
Three folders or style collage from Chapter 2
Style Journal
Computer with Internet access (optional)
Computer printer (optional)
Poster board and glue (optional)
Camera (optional)
Shopping budget

You've done an exceptional job of exploring your ideal style while keeping an eye on your current style, which means that you're moving rapidly toward the end goal: a highly personalized style that centers on your body, your tastes, and your lifestyle. So *that's* awesome. In order to transition seamlessly from how you look now to how you'd like to look, we're going to take one last glimpse at the work you've already done.

BACK TO THE FUTURE
As is often the case in life: you've gotta look back before moving forward. So rewind to all the work you did back in the days of Chapter 2. Grab any outfit photos, your inspiration

board or three folders of images, and your trusty Style Journal. Keeping in mind all of the Chapter 5 work pertaining to your *ideal* style, reread and reexamine your Chapter 2 thoughts and ideas about your *current* style.

Now ask yourself:

Where is the overlap? What do your current and ideal styles have in common? Colors, textures, or silhouettes? Use, comfort, or figure-flattery priorities? Brands, patterns, fabrics, go-to outfits? Look at all of your Chapter 2 writings. What can you bring from the past into the future and still feel quintessentially "you"? What of your old/current style can still work within your envisioned parameters for your new/ideal style?

Obviously the garments and accessories that remain in your ravaged wardrobe qualify as "overlappers." Everything hanging in your closet should fit within the parameters of your ideal wardrobe. However, you need to examine outfit assembly techniques, accessories, and the nuts and bolts of dressing aside from the tools themselves.

Based on what you wrote then and know now, which of your photographed/noted outfits align with your chosen stylistic direction? Can you identify why certain ensembles work and others don't? How can you retool the ones that are out of alignment?

How would you describe a style that melds your current and ideal styles? Start with ten adjectives and make sure they work both with the wardrobe workhorses hanging in your culled closet right now *and* the style you're envisioning for your future self. Reconsider everything you've learned about your style so far and see if you can encapsulate it in a single concise, descriptive phrase.

Or:

Fill in these blanks: Since my current style is _____, _____, and _____, yet my ideal style is _____, _____, and _____, the style I plan to create for myself will be _____, _____, and _____.

Revisit the steps you took in Chapter 2 but with an eye toward your new, refined look. Collect images of yourself in outfits that fit within your ideal style, or take new ones. Scour the web for photos of women whose styles align with your own, new priorities. Consider a new style icon for yourself. If it would be helpful, whip up a brand-new inspiration board.

Now, I SWEAR that shopping is imminent. But first, we've got to make a plan of consumer attack that encompasses both your sartorial present and fashion future. And in order to do that, you need to determine which purchases will be valuable, versatile, and expressive of your ideal style. That means figuring out what's missing.

THE HOLES

You're not gonna like this. No one ever does. But it is the absolute best way to assemble a targeted shopping list that will help you build your dream wardrobe.

In order to determine which pieces are missing from your current, thoroughly culled closet, you must spend at least two weeks assembling outfits from that closet. Using only what's in it now. Do not buy anything new, just work with what you've got. If you find that, miraculously, you've got everything you need already, pat yourself on the back—you're a minimalist. If you discover that you *really need* certain items, or can

pinpoint garments and accessories that would enhance or complete your outfits, take note. A true wardrobe hole-filler:

- **Suits multiple needs.** If you feel like a bright red belt would work perfectly with that one gray dress you've got, that's an interesting discovery. But not a need. If you feel like a bright red belt would complete three extremely diverse outfits, add it to the list.

- **Fits within your personal style.** I mean, obviously. But the thing about spending two-plus weeks wearing nothing but a handful of basic items is that it feels a little like a diet—you start craving things that you wouldn't ordinarily consider. Keep that in mind as you're identifying wardrobe holes. Make sure they all align with your ideal style.

- **Has staple potential.** Since you are in transition, focus on cake, not icing. You want to fill your wardrobe holes with items that have the potential to become true staples, meaning they are versatile, flattering, worn frequently, and central to your look. (See Chapter 5 for a refresher.)

Add items that fit all three criteria to a shopping list draft as you work your way through the two-week hole-identification period. You'll probably generate that list relatively quickly, so you'd better start thinking about how you're going to pay for all of these incoming duds.

BASICS OF BUDGETING

Personal finance is not my strong suit, but I absolutely cannot send you out to the shops without a few strong budgeting words. So here they are:

1. **Don't buy stuff you can't afford.** Affordable is relative, of course, but you should have some idea of your personal affordability parameters. If you're working on a grad student's budget and decide that a leather motorcycle jacket would fill several holes in you wardrobe, don't start scoping out a $3,000 Rick Owens purchase. There are multiple versions of just about every fashion item imaginable, and you can find an affordable one.

2. **Don't charge anything.** Ooooh, them's fightin' words. Don't care. I will never, ever condone using a credit card to purchase wardrobe items, *especially* planned wardrobe additions. Unless you've got one of those snappy cards that racks up airline miles and/or you pay off your balance every single month, save up the cash instead. There's nothing sexy about debt.

3. **Don't rush it.** Once you've assembled your list of potential purchases, you will want to run out to the nearest mall and shop until you have every single one of them in your hot little hands. Resist. You can have everything you want; you just can't have it all right away. Create a plan of action to slowly accumulate your list items. Here are some ways to spread the joy around:
   - Buy one item per pay period or per month.
   - Prioritize items by season. Buy what you can wear right now; wait to purchase items that won't be appropriate for six months.
   - Comparison shop. Price items online, try on any versions you can, and consider the pros and cons of various styles and materials.

4. Don't discount alternate means of procurement. If you're crafty, consider picking up a few patterns and some gorgeous cloth to make garments yourself. By all means, take your wish list to the thrift and consignment stores! No trend is truly new, and classic items endure, so you're bound to find affordable versions of the items you seek. And, should you be doing all this hard work around the holidays or a birthday, let friends and family know about your wish list for gift-giving purposes. Just make sure you request gift receipts from any obliging loved ones.

Again, every person will handle her disposable income differently, and I trust you won't do anything rash with your cash. But since the prospect of refreshing your depleted wardrobe undoubtedly clouds your head just a bit, I had to do the "voice of reason" thing right quick.

Oh. Actually? Gonna do it one last time.

Sewing your own garments is a great alternative to shopping. Patty sews much of her own wardrobe!

Patty, The Snug Bug
pattythesnugbug.com

SHOPPING SMART

As you prepare to shop for your new wardrobe items, take a moment to consider the pitfalls you may encounter along the way. There are many. And they are treacherous.

1. Buying something that almost fits.

Bottom line: just don't. Shop for your today-body, dress that body fabulously right now so that you can respect and celebrate yourself just as you are, and avoid clothes that fail to make you look and feel amazing. But since your head can get a bit foggy when those barely-able-to-button jeans are on clearance, here's your checklist:

- Ask yourself: Do I want this because my body is currently in flux? If so, won't there be something equally awesome once I've leveled out or reached my goal?
- Ask yourself: Can it be altered easily to fit properly? Figuring in the cost of alterations, is it worth it?
- Ask yourself: Are there workarounds? Is it a button-down shirt that won't button but can be worn over a tank top? If so, make sure there are at *least* three possible outfits in your closet that can utilize this piece.

2. Buying something you already own.

Hopefully you are now so intimately familiar with the contents of your closet that this is an impossibility. But in the heat of the moment, you may snap up an item with a twin already living in your closet. Here's your checklist:

- Before you shop, take inventory. Make a habit of it. Always.
- Ask yourself: How similar is this to my other _____s? (Insert item: dresses, boots, blazers, etc.) If it has three or more features in common with something you already own, leave it on the racks.
- Ask yourself: Do I love this because it's perfectly "me" or because it's incredibly familiar?

3. Buying something just because it's on sale.

This is the doozy, am I right? The "would I pay full price for this?" test is great in theory but often fails in practice. So try this instead:

- Ask yourself: What will happen if I don't buy this? Will I remember that I wanted it two weeks from now?
- Ask yourself: What about this item thrills me?
- Ask yourself: Can I envision at least three outfits that will work with this?

4. Buying something that you can't return.

Since you are shopping in transition, I must advise against buying anything that cannot be returned or exchanged. You've worked hard to hone this shopping list, but you may still make mistakes. However, should you stumble across a perfectly fitting, absolutely ideal item that happens to be marked "final sale," run through this checklist:

- Ask yourself: Is it completely free of flaws? Does it flatter me? Do I love it to pieces?
- Have a backup plan: consignment, a good friend or relative who wears your size, eBay.
- Ask yourself: If this fails to work for me, will I feel OK about trying to earn some of my money back or passing it along to someone else for free?

Shopping should be fun, of course, but it should also be strategic. Shopping regrets undoubtedly comprise the majority of items you purged or donated as you worked through the steps in this book. Why allow yourself to spend on subpar items that may eventually become regrets? Smart shopping is a skill worth cultivating. And now you've cultivated it. So let's get your butt to the mall.

STYLE JOURNAL SIDE NOTE: UTILIZATION

Finally, all that hard work is gonna pay off! You're headed out to buy some new duds—Style Journal in hand—ready to shop like a pro. But before you shop, consider reviewing what you wrote for:

- Chapter 2's style-centric questionnaire. Favorite brands, garment preferences, and loads of other relevant reminders can be found there.
- Chapter 3's defining physical traits and top ten best-loved body parts. Good reminders for a pre-shopping cram session.
- Chapter 5's synthesis of traits. Review the conclusions you drew while considering your current and ideal styles.

For easy reference as you shop, I suggest earmarking or flagging the following sections:

- Chapter 3's defining physical traits and top ten best-loved body parts. Because you want to shop for your today body and show off its best features with any new purchases.
- Chapter 4's figure-flattery tips. Which ones do you want to apply to yourself as you dress? You'll need to know when you shop!
- Chapter 5's list of priorities. You should consider comfort, color, use, and other factors should before purchasing anything.
- Chapter 6's list of wardrobe holes. Naturally, you'll want to bring this along.

KEEPIN' IT IDEAL

This is it—time to shop. Grab your list of items and make note of your current budget allotment. Bear in mind that you can buy some of the items that will fill your wardrobe holes but not all…unless you've saved a sizable chunk of change *and* have absolutely stellar shopping luck. There's nothing wrong with chipping away at that list month-by-month or paycheck-by-paycheck. If you're like most people, you've got more time than money, so take it slow.

Before you head out—or head to the computer to do some online shopping—grab your Style Journal. You need to evaluate every potential purchase on the criteria you established in Chapter 5. Here's a quick refresher to use as you consider each piece:

- **Does it fit your top use priority?** Washability? Versatility? Durability? Will this item *really* work for you?

- **Does it help you achieve one of your top three figure-flattery priorities?** If it hits on more than one, even better!

- **Does it fit your top comfort priority?** Consider your fussy feet, sensitive midsection, etc. How long will it take before this item irritates you physically?

- **Does it fit your color priorities?** If you're focusing on neutrals and need more of them, limit the brights. If you're working within a color scheme, think carefully about outliers. Also consider how patterns figure into your overall style.

- **How versatile is it?** Will it work for the office and the weekend? If creating continuity between work and weekend looks is a priority for you, the bulk of your new purchases should be versatile and flexible.

- **Can you describe it using the adjectives you designated for your ideal style?** Is it minimalist, romantic, Bohemian? Bold or classic? If not, reconsider.

- **Does it represent styles or silhouettes you've decided to avoid?** Does it fit within

90

aspects of your current style that you've committed to changing? It's extremely easy to purchase items that once worked within your current style but would now work against your ideal style. Again, do you love it because it's perfectly "you" or because it's incredibly familiar?

Some of these questions will be tough to answer if you're purchasing online, so check return policies. Just because it looks amazing on the gap.com model doesn't mean it'll look perfect on you. When your online purchases arrive on your front porch, try them on and evaluate them using the same criteria you'd use for an in-person purchase.

And I know this is a lot. If you bothered with the Style Journal Side Note earlier in this chapter, you might even believe I'm trying to suck all of the fun out of shopping. But think of this exercise as a grocery store run: you're stocking up on items that you *need* as opposed to cherry picking items that you merely *want*. You should come home with armloads of flattering, versatile stuff that suits you perfectly. What you buy now and in your next few rounds of shopping may not feel exciting, but the items you evaluate and purchase will quickly become workhorses. And they'll make you feel chic, sophisticated, and pulled-together in ways that your

old garments never could have. And those alluringly pretty but undeniably impractical items? The ones that sang you a siren song as you scoured the mall for pleated skirts and V-neck sweaters? Most likely, they would have become closet orphans in a matter of months.

As you chip away at your list of wardrobe holes and spend some time living within the boundaries of your newly defined style, you will begin to internalize many of your Style Journal notes and insights. Eventually you'll glance at a garment or accessory, run through your personal mental checklist, and decide in moments if it will work for you. *That* is when you can start adding some frosting to your primarily cake shopping list—when you have synthesized what you've learned, made any necessary adjustments, and feel like you're truly walking the talk.

Speaking of which, let's consider how to fold these new purchases into your ever-morphing wardrobe.

SMOOTHING THE TRANSITION

It's unlikely that you're moving from a wardrobe comprised of pantsuits and stilettos to one that relies heavily on maxi skirts and hip-slung belts. Nevertheless, you should consider how to best utilize your new items while still keeping the old staples in rotation. It might surprise you to hear that maintaining three lists will help.

1. **Keep a running list of newly purchased items.** Since you've been in acquisition mode, it's possible that you lost track of what you procured and what remains on the list, especially if you throw a few bonus, nonessential items into the mix. So keep a list. Whenever you buy or order something new, add it to the list. Keep a section in your Style Journal for this purpose so that you can find all of your style-related info in one place.

2. **Keep a running list of underutilized items.** You're unlikely to have a lot of languishing garments early on. Having just brutally purged your closet, you'll need to make use of all remaining items and all new ones as well. But, eventually, some pieces will fall into disuse. Note them in your Style Journal. You'll find a list of seldom-worn garments helpful in the long run because you should also…

3. **Keep a running list of potential outfits.** One of the absolute best ways to keep your style evolution on track is to generate an outfit list. Set aside a few hours each month to rummage through your closet and jot down ideas for potential outfits. To jump-start the process, look at your lists of new and underutilized items and craft outfits around those pieces. Then work your way through your wardrobe until you've got a hefty list of options. As you move outfits from paper to person, take note of which ones work, which ones don't, and why.

These three lists will help you now—as you ease into your revised, ideal style—by giving you the tools to fold new purchases into daily wear. These three lists will remain helpful tools once your style has gelled a bit more by encouraging you to mind your inventory and keep everything you own in rotation. I've maintained new, underutilized, and outfit lists for more than three years, and they've proven absolutely invaluable in keeping my style from stagnating.

Although these tools will undoubtedly help you move toward your ideal style in theory, practice may seem a bit bumpy. Feel free to tweak and revise your goals as you learn more about what truly works for you in daily life, but also remember that anything new will take some getting used to. Keep experimenting, don't give up, and give yourself some time and space to let your style unfold organically.

Consider talking with trusted friends and family members about your experience in revising your personal style, and explain what it means to you. This can help if your social group will likely question any visible sartorial shifts. It helps to have a few buddies who know the whole story and who can support you should the queries become overwhelming or invasive. Articulating your reasons for making these changes and how you expect those changes to affect you can also help you mentally summarize your experience. You've done so much on your own; now consider sharing what you've learned with others.

Fabienne, The House in the Clouds
thehouseintheclouds.com

TAKE YOUR TIME

Well, my dear, we've come to the point in our journey where I nudge you out of the nest and let you spread your wings. You've got the knowledge, the tools, and the desire. Now you just need to dive right in and live it for a while. I recommend that you continue writing in your Style Journal as you discover new garments, tactics, and figure-flattery priorities, taking any notes that seem relevant. Then, after about three months of living with and tinkering with your revised style, ask yourself:

Lisa, Respect the Shoes
respecttheshoes.blogspot.com

1. **How do I feel about my look?** Is it working? Do you feel more confident, powerful, and beautiful? If not all the time, most of the time? Are you comfortable? Do you feel like yourself?

2. **What feedback have I gotten?** This is a tough one since observers may react to any and all change with unwelcome curiosity. Additionally, most people in your social circle are unlikely to say, "I liked your old style better." And thank goodness for that. But consider the feedback you've received that you consider to be both honest and heartfelt. What has drawn the most comments? Did you agree with the observations of others? Anything surprising?

3. **What do I need to tweak?** It's extremely unlikely that you got everything perfect on the first go-around. If you did, kudos to you! If you didn't, any idea what needs

altering? Do you need more flat shoes, fewer skirts, more color? Did you pick any items as wardrobe staples that you simply haven't worn?

4. **Do I need to add anything to my wardrobe hole list?** Careful, now. Follow the same meticulous steps as you did in your first shopping excursions to avoid adding superfluous items to your wardrobe. And beware the trap of constant shopping! Focus on items that you know from experience would make your sartorial life easier.

After you've given these questions some thought, make a plan of action. You may need to purge and donate a few items, and they may be relatively new. That's just fine. This is a long-term learning experience, and it can be hard to accurately predict which pieces will work for you in the long term. You may need to generate some new outfit ideas based on a revised style direction, or seek out some duplicates of your most-used items. Ask questions, identify problems, and formulate solutions. You've got all of the tools you need now and can continue to hone and adjust your style on your own.

And that is FANTASTIC.

Endgame: Love

I've heard many people say that confidence is key to great style, and I agree. But I'm inclined to believe that embarking upon a personal style journey has more to do with trust. And my hope is that after plowing through a truly massive amount of introspection, exploration, and work, you have built some trust.

As a stylish woman, you must trust that you—and only you—know what looks and feels best on your unique body. Plenty of people will have opinions, and some of them may contradict your own instincts, but in the end, you're the decision maker. Trust yourself. You know best.

As a stylish woman, you must trust that you can make sound decisions about what will work for your life and lifestyle. Sure, there may be more traditionally flattering, sexier, flashier options that would boost your fashion cachet, and some people may nudge you toward those options. But you know yourself, you know how you want to look, and, most importantly, you know why. Trust yourself. You know best.

As a stylish woman, you must trust that you can create and hone your personal style. Style evolves constantly. You may feel as though you've just completed a journey, but you've really just begun. And that is marvelous! As you learn more about your body, your beauty, your tastes, and how you want to present your physical form to the observing world, you'll gradually refine your style accordingly. And although there will be bumps and misfires and the occasional disastrous outfit, you'll still know better than anyone how to move your style forward. Trust yourself. You know best.

Once you've built a foundation of trust, you'll find that your blossoming personal style is an unmatched vehicle for self-expression. As I mentioned waaaay back in the introduction, comportment, demeanor, dress, grooming, and overall appearance constitute the first levels of information about ourselves that we offer to the observing world. They may not be the most important, but they are the first, which makes them worthy of effort and attention. People are going to see you every day, and they're going to see you clothed. Why not take the opportunity to utilize style, clothing, grooming, and accessorizing to show those people who you are and what you love about your body? Why not view your style as an aspect of your projected self? Why not express yourself through dress? When you make choices that reflect your tastes and showcase your luminous beauty, you broadcast self-knowledge, self-respect, and confidence. Never let anyone tell you that style is unimportant, shallow, or frivolous. There is nothing frivolous about self-expression, under any guise.

To be honest, though, the trust and self-expression are just by-products. The real endgame is love. The point of all this rumination and exploration and change is to cultivate love for your body and personality and essential self. Self-care is absolutely integral to self-love, and while self-care can take infinite forms, I believe that personal style is a marvelous way to train yourself to steward your body. After all, style is a form of self-care that can be enacted daily. So many people view dressing as a chore, a bother, another irritating task that impedes the day's events. But dressing can be a love song to your fabulous figure! It can be fun and expressive and exciting and bold and invigorating and creative. It can be a way to remind yourself that beauty and power live inside you and should be honored.

There is an undeniable and powerful connection between how you look and how you feel. You deserve to look and feel amazing, and you can. Because no matter what you wear or how you wear it or how different you may look from the fashion magazines, you are already pretty. You always have been.

And don't you forget it.

About the Author

Sally McGraw is a Minneapolis-based freelance writer, blogger, teacher, and communications professional. She earned a creative writing degree from Binghamton University in 1998 and, after graduation, worked in the book and magazine publishing industry for ten years. She has contributed writing to local newspapers, magazines, and websites throughout her entire professional life.

In addition to writing her popular daily style and body image blog Already Pretty, she has contributed to The Frisky, typeF, and Glamour and is an ongoing features contributor to the Minneapolis StarTribune. She offers personal shopping and style consultation services, both in person for clients living in the Twin Cities and via e-mail for clients worldwide. She is one-third of Strong, Sexy, & Stylish, a collective of experts working to teach women to love themselves.

Sally spoke on a panel at BlogHer 2012 and taught a workshop at the 2011 Independent Fashion Bloggers Evolving Influence Conference. She has also taught workshops at the University of Minnesota and classes via local community education programs.

Visit **www.alreadypretty.com** for more information about Sally, to participate in online forums related to this book, and to purchase a companion PDF.

26218041R00060

Made in the USA
Charleston, SC
31 January 2014